JOURNAL with THREAD

JOURNAL with THREAD

A practical guide to sewing seasonal stories
in fabric & thread with iron-on transfers

Jessie Chorley

DAVID & CHARLES

www.davidandcharles.com

Contents

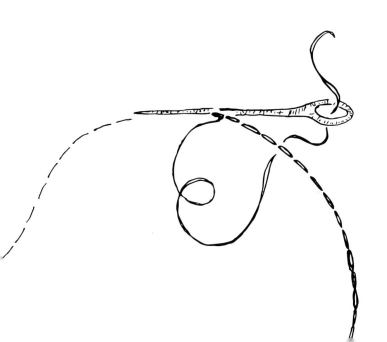

Introduction

Welcome to my seasonal, slow-stitching project, *Journal with Thread*. The fabric journal, which we will make in the pages ahead, is a celebration of my love for collecting fabric, thread and other personal memorabilia and treasures. It focuses on my signature style of hand-embroidery, and my unique approach to simple patching and appliqué techniques.

This book is a guide to making your own stitched fabric journal. I have laid out how to do this step by step, providing clear, technical details at every stage. However, as both a maker and a teacher, I always encourage a free and intuitive approach to crafting – I don't believe in rigidly following rules or instructions, and what you make with your hands must always come from the heart. I have been guided by this belief while creating this book.

This project is rooted in the approach I take to making my own embroidered artworks, especially fabric storybooks and memory journals, which are crafted from preloved and found materials. It features my hand-drawn stitch guides and will also explain my favourite embroidery techniques – and, to inspire, guide and prompt you, I will refer to these guides throughout the book.

Journal with Thread is a project suitable for all skill levels. If you are a beginner, you can follow the instructions in this book as near to the letter as you wish. However, if you are an experienced maker, and wish to embrace your own style, feel free to take your own approach to making your stitched journal, and not be inhibited by the instructions in this book.

I encourage you to take inspiration from my thrifty, re-purposing, make-do-and-mend approach to crafting. Dig deep and try to make this project from fabrics and threads that you may already have. Take inspiration from your collection of materials as you build your own unique seasonal fabric journal. For me, working in this fashion has been so liberating. My hope is that you will enjoy it too.

What is a fabric journal?

For me, a fabric journal is a very familiar and comforting thing. I started making fabric books from a very young age. Stitching and getting creatively lost in the never-ending world of making fabric books has been a part of my life for as long as I can remember.

I first made a fabric journal under my mum's watchful eye. I grew up in a family of makers in the hills of rural north Wales, where there was a strong emphasis on 'make do and mend' and on using the materials we had to hand as our starting point. These early years, making things with my hands and with my family, formed the basis of the life that I now live as a textile artist, tutor and author. It's with these early life memories in mind that I have designed this seasonal slow stitch guide.

Slow stitching

Crafting a stitched fabric book from start to finish should ideally be a slow, mindful exercise, something that you work on over time, far away from the fast pace of modern life. Building this seasonal journal might just help to slow things down and can bring you to a more peaceful and creative place in your busy life.

A fabric book can be made in any size and from pretty much any thrifted fabric. For this project we are focusing on the four seasons, but fabric books can be made and then filled to hold the memories of many different stories and of cherished life events.

Once you enter the world of making stitched books the possibilities are endless. Books can be made to remember a loved one, to welcome a new family member or to celebrate a particular life journey or event. You could even make a stitched recipe book.

Stitched journals can be used like regular paper books, and worked in daily for keeping notes, ideas, words and stories. You can easily pin or even stitch little scrappy paper items into your fabric pages as mementoes. This works well with travel tickets, photos and other memorabilia.

These days, I usually start by constructing the book and then embellish it at the next stage. My fabric books are always made using thrifted and found fabric. I like to live with my newly constructed books around me for several months, or even years, before I finally start the slow and mindful process of filling them with my stories in stitch, fabric and odd found objects. I cherish the collection of handmade fabric books that I have crafted over my life; each one tells a different story and reminds me of a particular time in my life.

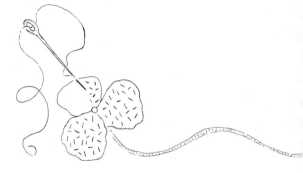

About this book

This book will show you how to make and embellish a fabric journal from start to finish. It will guide you step by step through the process of stitching the basic journal, using different embroidery stitches, and giving advice on following your own creative path and where to look for inspiration.

The central theme of this project is the four seasons: Spring, Summer, Autumn and Winter. At the back of this book, you will find four hand-drawn transfers, one dedicated to each season. The four seasonal motifs are accompanied by four additional transfers, which you can use for the cover pages of your journal. There is also a large selection of smaller templates for you to use as you wish throughout the project. There are illustrations of fun motifs as well as my signature alphabets and number designs.

One of the transfer designs is a pin cushion. The pin cushion is intended for the inside back cover of the journal and is designed as a final-page project; think of it as a shrine to your love of stitching. It can be embellished in full before being lightly padded and used as a practical pin cushion or keepsake space at the back of your fabric journal.

Introducing fabric journals

The first part of this book will introduce you to the concept of fabric books and explore the role they've played in my life and work, as well as talking about where to seek inspiration. I also talk about where to find 'treasure' – those special notions, findings, keepsakes, fabrics and threads that can be built into a collection by hunting them out in markets, thrift stores and even in your own attic.

Guides to embroidery stitches and appliqué will give you a great idea of the different textures and details that can be stitched into your journal.

Making your journal

Before you start to embellish the transfer designs, you will need to create your basic fabric journal. You can choose whether to make the journal first and then embellish it, or whether to make the flat embellished panels first and then use these to construct the fabric book. Either way, your finished fabric journal will measure 20 x 20cm (8 x 8in). Full step-by-step instructions with clear photos will guide you through the process of making the fabric journal, leaving you free to then embark on the creative process of filling it.

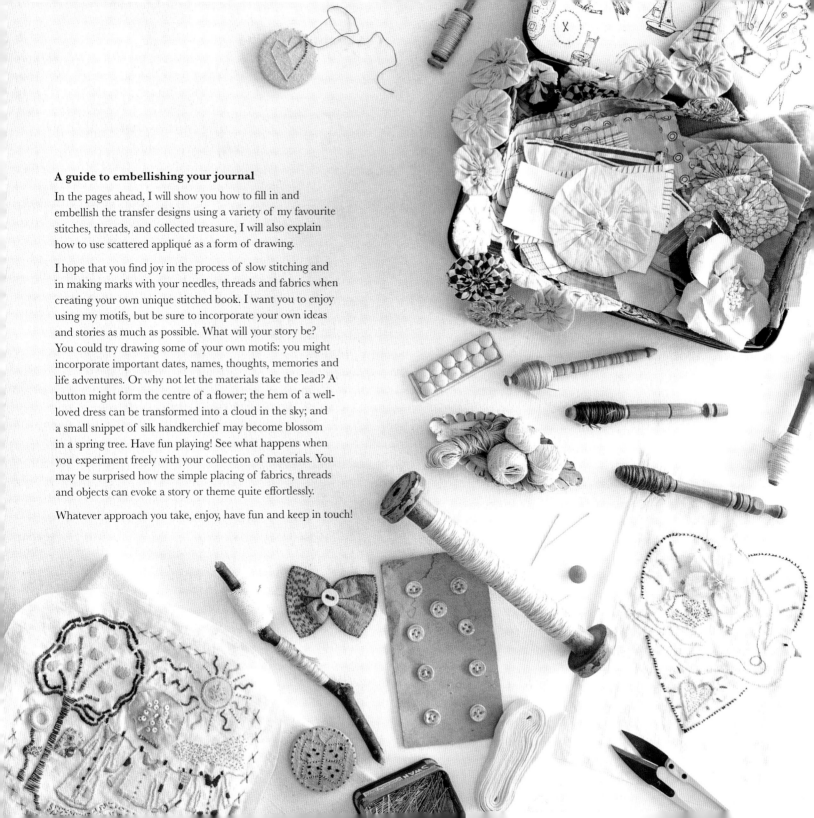

A guide to embellishing your journal

In the pages ahead, I will show you how to fill in and embellish the transfer designs using a variety of my favourite stitches, threads, and collected treasure, I will also explain how to use scattered appliqué as a form of drawing.

I hope that you find joy in the process of slow stitching and in making marks with your needles, threads and fabrics when creating your own unique stitched book. I want you to enjoy using my motifs, but be sure to incorporate your own ideas and stories as much as possible. What will your story be? You could try drawing some of your own motifs: you might incorporate important dates, names, thoughts, memories and life adventures. Or why not let the materials take the lead? A button might form the centre of a flower; the hem of a well-loved dress can be transformed into a cloud in the sky; and a small snippet of silk handkerchief may become blossom in a spring tree. Have fun playing! See what happens when you experiment freely with your collection of materials. You may be surprised how the simple placing of fabrics, threads and objects can evoke a story or theme quite effortlessly.

Whatever approach you take, enjoy, have fun and keep in touch!

Inspiration and sourcing

Before you start your journal, and throughout the process, gather together materials and inspiration to use during the making period. This is a free and intuitive way of approaching both collecting and making – find out where it leads you.

Try to be climate conscious and thrifty when sourcing and gathering materials. Personally, I don't favour buying online from large retailers, I prefer to stumble across inspiration and materials during my travels. The best treasure and inspiration can often be found at very unexpected times.

Become familiar with your neighbourhood: join a swapping group, visit thrift stores, go to car-boot sales, rummage through garage and yard sales. Enjoy staying offline and find inspiration in person rather than on the internet. Check out what events are happening when you travel next. Most cities have good markets where treasure can be found. As do small, rural villages. Ask family members and you may be surprised what is available to use from your family's collection of tablecloths, linens etc. Materials with a personal or family connection are always the best inspiration.

What makes good treasure?

As you rummage through thrift shops, markets and your family's stash you will soon come across both inspirational and useful materials. Make the invisible visible, and cherish and celebrate found items in your stitched journal. Reimagine, deconstruct and reconstruct found fabrics. It's amazing what material you can gather from cutting up an old shirt. Silk ties hold many layers of interesting fabric. Work your found fabrics, cuffs, buttons, hems and collars into your story and into your fabric journal.

Collect odd bits of jewellery, charms, lace, ribbons, parts of old watches, paper thread spools, little pearl buttons, beads, sequins, old postcards, vintage haberdashery, old thimbles, decorative scissors, beautiful wooden spools, vintage threads, preloved fabric, snippets of vintage quilts, vintage paper or silk flowers, sequins and small glass beads.

Bear in mind that preloved fabrics and objects will often trigger memories. A snippet from a worn dress, a collar from a favourite shirt, or a patch from an old quilt cover or beloved cushion cover can all carry personal associations. So focus on selecting items that will both inspire you and spark a unique narrative, either for you or for the person you are making your fabric journal for.

Take pride in your collection

Take pride and enjoy displaying and arranging your inspirations, tools and materials. I have gathered vintage wooden spools for years and they now show off a lot of my favourite threads. They also look gorgeous on display!

Whenever I buy new thread I wind it onto one of these vintage wooden spools, or a paper version. I also use them to hold an array of odd threads, string, lace and ribbons. They live in my work basket or on shelves at home and in my studio, and they often come travelling with me. In my work box they become part of my life and they are familiar friends. Use what you have close to home – little wooden sticks from the garden are also great for winding threads onto. I am always gathering them on my walks to the studio.

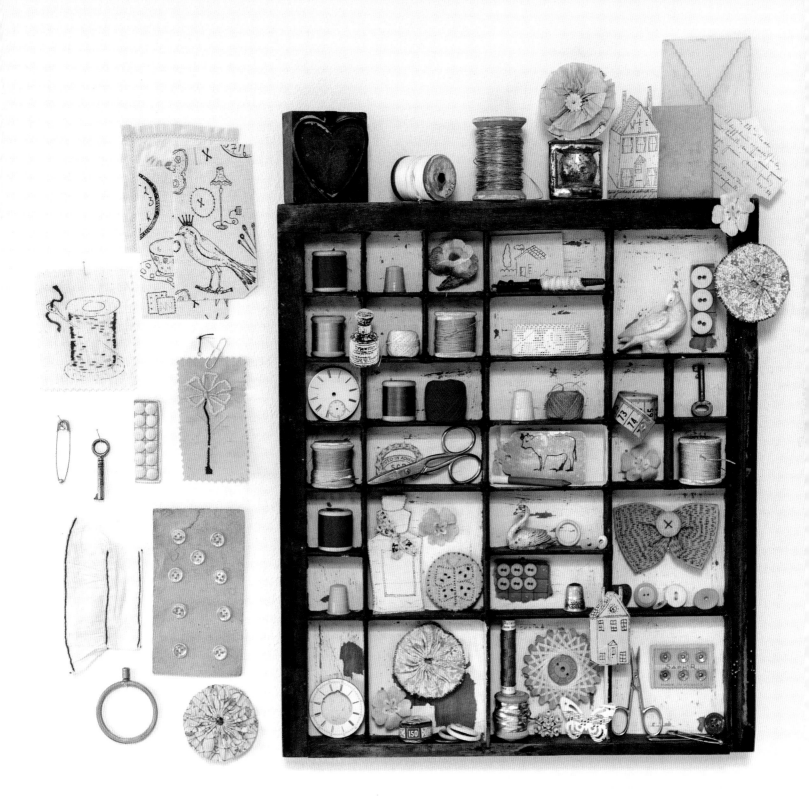

Keeping a sketchbook

Getting into the habit of keeping a journal or sketchbook is a must for this type of stitch project. Sketchbooks are beautiful, rich idea banks that we can revisit again and again over time. It is like viewing your inner creative thoughts or speaking to an inspiring old friend.

Don't be precious about your sketchbooks. Fill them, write in them, draw in them. Use them for all those random ideas that jump into your mind in the middle of the night, or on a long walk.

Journalling and sketchbooking are so useful because you can take a jumble of messy thoughts and put them down onto a page quickly, either in words or as a quick mark or drawing. Revisit these ideas if you hit a creative block. We all live busy, modern lives, and it's nice to have somewhere offline to house precious keepsakes and ideas. Fabric scraps can be pinned to paper pages for inspiration or as reminders of what you have in your personal stash, as can snippets of threads, tapes, ribbons and lace.

Tip: Even though digital smartphones and note-taking apps are great, let's try and stay away from the digital world while we make this project together – fill a sketchbook instead, or fill several!

Look around for inspiration

Nature has always been an influence on my work: plants and trees from local London parks; the Thames riverbank and its ever-changing wildlife; my travels to the Swiss mountains; and cherished plants from my mum's garden in Wales all appear in my work a lot. So take advantage of your own garden by drawing it throughout the year as you delve deep into making your own seasonal stitched journal. If you don't have a garden, head to the park to gather and draw plants and flowers during your seasonal journey.

Aside from the natural world, take inspiration from your surroundings by recording or sketching those, too.

- Draw favourite objects from around your home
- Sketch objects in your local museum or gallery
- Make a quick outline drawing of your pets!
- Write down small snippets of significant personal conversations, memories, dates, important things that happen from season to season with family and beloved friends
- Use a treasured family recipe book as your inspiration – passed down recipes are great as seasonal inspiration
- Include a favourite drawing, seasonal poem, or quote

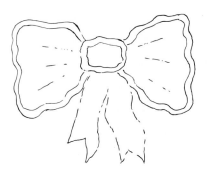

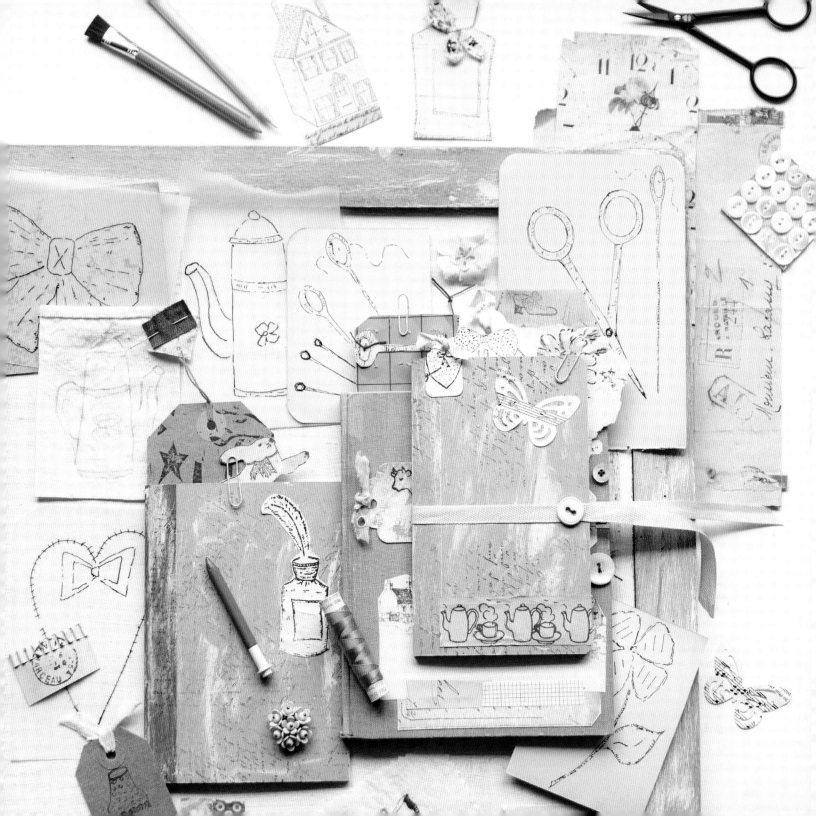

Tools and materials

Before starting your fabric journal spend some time gathering your tools and materials. Below is a list of items that I use regularly when constructing a fabric book. Be thrifty and try and use what you have close to hand – this is very much my approach to making. I hope the list below helps you on your creative journey.

Work box or container: Let's start our journey by being organized. Choose a container to house your materials and tools while you're working on this seasonal project. Your fabric journal in progress could also be kept in such a container. Look out for something pre-used and beautiful to the eye. This could be a vintage tin, box or basket. I prefer vintage sweet or soap tins and small vintage suitcases are my weakness! I always clean tins, boxes and baskets before use, and find great joy in lining them with pretty fabrics and papers. Enjoy customizing your finds. Add a padded or fabric cushion to the inside of the lid of a biscuit tin. This will instantly make your box or tin useful, and you'll enjoy keeping your crafting tools, needles and threads in such a beautiful and practical item.

Base fabric for journal: What will you make your fabric journal from? Choose a base fabric that will evoke a memory or narrative for you, the maker – vintage tablecloths, tray cloths, hankies and linen napkins are all perfect base materials. I suggest using items made solely from natural fabrics as they are easier to embellish using embroidery, mending and patching techniques. Select fabrics that can be cut down to 44 x 44cm (17¼ x 17¼in).

Base fabric for transfers: You could transfer your motifs directly onto your journal before working on them, but I suggest you transfer your motifs onto separate fabrics and build them up first, as separate little artworks, before attaching them to your journal. All of my motifs were transferred onto fabric from a collection of vintage white cotton napkins. It's best to use natural fabrics only, and finely woven fabric is best, so that the transfers will attach neatly.

Pin cushion: I always use a fresh pin cushion when starting a new big project. This helps keep things organized if you are working on several stitching projects at once. The pin cushion will become full, busy and messy, it will be your base not just for pins and needles, but also for all those small, odd fabric scraps, buttons and threads.

Sketchbook: A sketchbook or paper journal for note taking, designing and gathering information and inspiration for your journal. Sketch your own motifs and take direct inspiration from your personal surroundings. Enjoy filling your book in advance or at the same time as working on your journal project.

Pink and white tailors' chalk pencils: I use these regularly to mark my ideas directly onto my fabric, as they work well on different coloured surfaces. They are less damaging than synthetic pens, and better for the environment.

2B graphite pencil: Always useful for tracing in combination with a light box and tracing paper. I also regularly use a pencil for drawing directly onto fabrics before sewing over the pencil marks.

Erasable pens: There are several types of erasable pen on the market, so choose a good quality brand. The selection of colours available in this type of pen is useful for marking designs on different shades and types of fabric.

Flexible rubber thimble: Rubber thimbles are flexible and really help with pushing a needle through thick edges of fabric. The rubber does not restrict the movement of your fingers when sewing.

Long tailors' pins: I simply love these long metal pins. I would be lost without them. They can be used to hold fabrics in place at any stage of the making process, and they don't have plastic or glass ends so you can freely iron over them.

Double-ended needle threader: This is a great little tool for helping to thread your needle.

Tape measure: I tend to use paper or fabric dressmakers' tapes, they are more practical than metal ones.

Beautiful preloved tools: I lay these items down directly on my base fabric, then draw around them with a pencil. Very quickly you will have a neat little drawing to use as a template. Enjoy filling the design with stitches of your choice. This is a top secret tip!

DMC embroidery needles: I always use DMC embroidery needles in sizes 1-3. They are strong, sharp and have big eyes for easy threading.

Embroidery hoop: Embroidery hoops help with tension when embroidering fabrics. I don't use hoops a lot, apart from when I am stitching on very fine silk fabrics, but please feel free to use a hoop if you are used to working in this way.

Iron: You'll need an iron for both ironing fabrics and also for attaching transfers. I prefer a small hand-size iron. Little irons are very practical when crafting smaller items like this project.

Wool ironing mats: These are flexible and let you carry your work around on them, like a tray. You can iron onto them and they are great to keep ongoing projects on. They come in a variety of sizes and are available worldwide. You can also stick your pins and needles into them when working. I have several at my studio for different projects.

Eco filling or padding: I prefer using preloved and recycled fabric for padding fabric books wherever possible. A piece of boiled and felted wool blanket or jumper is a very practical option for adding a thicker, inner layer to pages and covers.

A beeswax bar: This is useful for helping to prevent knotting in threads and is an absolute must in my craft box. Run your thread lightly across the wax just once, and add more when needed.

Wire snips or small pliers: Use these for deconstructing vintage finds, metal buttons, bits of clock, odd bits of jewellery, etc.

Small metal hammer: This can be used for flattening buckles and jewellery. Making these items flatter will help when stitching them onto your work.

Scissors: Large tailors' scissors for cutting your fabric and small snips or scissors for threads and trimming back fabric ends.

Tracing paper: Use tracing paper and a graphite pencil when tracing designs.

Personal ephemera: Anything that evokes memories, such as old charms, buttons, vintage lace and ribbons, small keys etc, all of which can be stitched into your work. Rummage through your drawers at home or ask family and friends.

Preloved and vintage fabric scraps: Use some favourite items from your personal collection for this project, or source preloved fabrics in advance just for this journal. Focus on using fabrics that evoke a personal narrative; this will give your work a truly personal touch. This project is great for using up those tiny scraps that we all love to save! Be mindful when choosing your fabric that although colourful, busy fabrics are a delight to work with, plainer pieces will give you the option to work back into them at a later date, with stitched words and illustrations.

Wadding (stuffing): A sheep's wool wadding or natural kapok stuffing for padding appliqué shapes. Personally, I prefer kapok stuffing because it's light and you can push it right into fiddly little areas.

Wooden darning mushroom: This simple tool is very useful to use when darning and mending holes in preloved fabrics. I use a vintage wooden one. Have a look in your local thrift store or find a new one in your local craft store. The mushroom is placed inside or under your fabric with the worn area stretched over the top of the mushroom. You can use an elastic band or piece of string to hold your fabric in place. You will now be easily able to darn and fix the worn area in the fabric.

Choosing and using threads

Gathering thread is a constant process for me, which goes hand-in-hand with my life as an embroidery artist. The act of sourcing threads makes me incredibly satisfied and inspired; like a painter choosing their paint. I hope this guide to thread will help, inspire and encourage you. Become familiar with thread. Let collecting it become part of your creative process. Seek out thread that sparks joy.

DMC embroidery threads

For this project's colour scheme, I have chosen thirteen shades of DMC Mouliné Spécial embroidery thread and five shades of DMC Coton Perlé embroidery thread. These colours are what I commonly use when making my own version of this seasonal journal. Feel free to take inspiration from my choices and use a similar palette, or go about selecting your own. You can add as many colours to the project as you like, or change them up as much as you want. Please don't feel that you have to stick to the shades that I have selected. You will find the colour codes for my chosen DMC threads at the back of this book. Alternatively, you could use any other brand of similar thread.

Using DMC Mouliné Spécial embroidery thread

This thread is designed for embroidery and comes in six divisible strands. Dividing the strands allows you to vary the weight of your stitches. I mainly stitch with either one or two strands. If you would like to build up your designs more quickly, try using two, three or even four strands at one time. How many strands we use really is down to personal preference. Refer to my 'Stitch guides' for further guidance.

Practise playing and sewing with one strand first and then add more strands. Have fun experimenting before starting on your final work. You will soon discover the possibilities are quite endless. It's also worth noting that DMC Mouliné Spécial thread is colour-fast.

Using DMC Coton Perlé embroidery thread

This cotton thread is an absolute favourite of mine for bold and juicy looking stitching. I always use it in thickness No. 8, which is the mid-range thickness. Unlike DMC Mouliné Spécial thread, this thread is not designed to be split or divided; you will be stitching with the entire thickness. It is great for so many stitches, and because of its thickness it will build up quickly and give speedy results. I use this thread a lot as a base when I am creating couched work. Try out some favourite stitches and see how you get on with it. DMC Coton Perlé thread is also colour-fast. You can use any other brand of similar thread, in a similar thickness and style, and vintage crochet cottons also work just as well.

Collecting vintage threads

I strongly advise combining old or varied threads from your own stash with the brand-new DMC thread that I have recommended. Be thrifty and inventive. If you are anything like me, you will have a vast and random collection of odd threads purchased over months and years. I am constantly buying different threads for certain projects, but also sometimes purely for the joy of feeling them and proudly owning them. Yes, I am a hoarder of beautiful threads!

Look close to home when selecting threads for this project. Rummage in those boxes and drawers, and use up those last tiny bits of thread. This will make your fabric journal both personal to you and unique. I have a large jar in my studio and I always put odd lengths of thread into it when I am busy sewing; this is the time to use such odd and precious threads. Swapping threads with like-minded others is also a fun pastime of mine.

Threads for bold couching

When creating bold, stand-alone shapes and raised details using couching, you can use pretty much anything you choose as a base thread: string, wool, embroidery thread, ribbon, thin rope, a rolled strip of fabric. When using thinner base threads, I like to stitch them loosely through my base fabric first, in big and very close together running stitches before anchoring the running stitches neatly in place with small, straight whip stitches. Enjoy finding odd and interesting threads to experiment with to achieve bold couching details. The odder the better is what I say when it comes to base materials!

NOTE: I have used couching a lot in my journal. The most prominent examples are where I have couched down a strip of folded ivory silk fabric to the base of my pin cushion design (on the inside back cover), and on the Winter page, where I have couched down two strands of fine jute string to represent the lawn outside the festive house. On the Autumn page, I couched down two strands of jute string to create the grass effect under the house, but this time the couched string flows off the embroidered panel and onto the rest of the journal's page.

Creating variegated threads

Mixing strands of different coloured thread is something I do a lot in my work, and I encourage you to try it. You will be threading both strands of thread through one needle and stitching the two colours together to create a mottled and variegated look, so take care when choosing the types of thread you want to mix together. For best results, combine two strands of DMC Mouliné thread in two highly contrasting colours. This technique works best with satin stitch and long seed stitch. You will see that I have done this a lot in my seasonal journal. Look at the tree trunks on the Summer and Winter pages. Also, the border on the front cover heart design is built up using variegated thread, as is the beautiful bow on the back page of my journal.

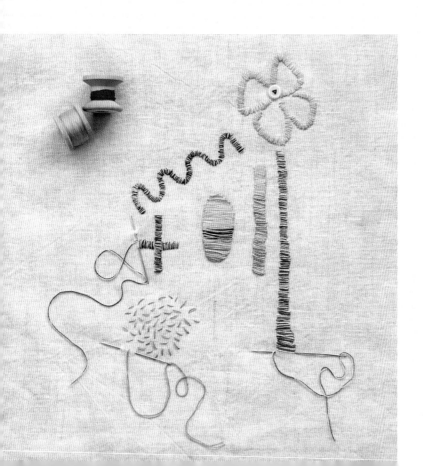

Correct thread length

An arm's length of thread is my favoured length to work with. For most embroidery projects this is perfect. Avoid working with very long thread as it will likely knot, strain your arms and you will end up wasting a lot of your precious threads.

Treating thread with beeswax

Adding beeswax to thread helps to prevent knots forming. I find it also helps when I work satin stitch using two strands of DMC Mouliné thread. Keep a bar of beeswax in your crafting kit at all times and simply run your threads across it. Don't be too heavy-handed with the application, just run the thread across the wax bar lightly once and add more when needed. In warmer climates keep your beeswax in the fridge so it doesn't become too soft. And take care, soft wax may rub off onto your fabric and leave marks.

Beeswax to help thread your needle

A beeswax bar can also be amazingly helpful if you are struggling with threading thicker, silky and springy threads though the eye of your needle. Be generous with the wax application and apply it just to the tip of your chosen thread. Cut the tip of your waxed thread with a sharp pair of scissors at a slight angle. You should now be able to push your thread through the eye of your needle.

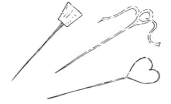

Stitching words and numbers

When embroidering words, names and dates I use either simple back stitch or fine couching. When working fine couched lettering in my journal, I used one strand of DMC Mouliné thread (colour 924) to lay down a base thread, and then used one strand of the same thread to work very tiny straight stitches over my original base thread. This creates very fine, raised lettering. You can come back to your letters once all the main shapes have been stitched and add dashes of colour to individual letters. Dot 'i's with a different colour, or cross 't's with a contrasting colour, just as I have done in my Rosette design on the back cover of my journal.

The way you place words in your book is important, so make sure you do this mindfully. Words can be central to your book's design, but also don't let them take over from your main seasonal design. I prefer small areas of text, so they become precious. You could stitch words on patches of fabric and appliqué them into your journal at a later date. Practice first on your doodle cloth (see Doodle cloths)!

A note on needles

Which needles we favour as stitchers is very much down to personal preference. I nearly always use DMC embroidery needles in sizes 1-3. I use these needles because they have very sharp points for fine embroidery, and they are not too small to hold in your fingers. They are also very strong and therefore good for thicker areas of fabric like seams and borders. They have a large eye for easy threading and they are long enough for me to use the tip as a tucking-under tool when I am working on small and fiddly appliqué details.

I also have a vast collection of old, large steel needles, which are great for thick threads, strings, gold threads etc. Don't struggle with tiny needles, use something that you can thread and that feels stable in your fingers. Finding the needle or brand of needles that works perfectly for you will make embroidery a delight to do.

Appliqué guide

Appliqué involves cutting out fabric shapes and then stitching them to a base fabric. The stitches can be small and almost invisible, or you can work in colourful stitches that are celebrated and become part of your overall design. I refer to my style of appliqué as needle- or finger-turned, because, like many of us, I use my fingers and/or the sharp end of my embroidery needle to tuck the fiddly fabric edges under, to create a neat edge before I stitch them down to my base fabric.

Appliqué may simply be scattered in small clusters across your work or along a border, but it is often used to build up an entire design, working slowly, layer by layer, scrap by scrap. It is a beautiful way to create a patchwork quilt, when it is known as crazy patchwork. Appliqué can also be a perfect method for mending holes in clothing and other worn fabric.

Try combining appliqué with rows of small, densely packed running stitches that flow in a variety of different directions to add not just beautiful detail but also to strengthen your finished work.

Adding appliqué to your journal

Scattered appliqué details can be added at any stage of your making journey. Think of this way of working as a form of drawing and mark making. I keep small scraps of pre-ironed and cut fabric by my side at all times when sewing. You may find that adding fabric patches to your premade journal early on will really inspire you.

Starting with adding scattered appliqué to your project is a great way to jump forward with a project like this. Especially if you are feeling a bit stuck or overwhelmed. Consider filling some of your motifs with small areas of appliqué before you start the main decorative stitching. I have taken this approach a lot on my seasonal pages. On the Summer page, early on I laid down my grassy lawn by taking a piece of fine white fabric and scrunching it up as I attached it to create a wavy, folded effect. It's held down with small, scattered straight seed stitches.

In the base of the Pin Cushion design, I appliquéd a small section of a soft pink vintage tape measure. Instantly this brought the design together, in a fun way that celebrates my love of collecting.

The raised blue cloud on my Autumn page was appliquéd using a snippet from a blue silk dress sleeve cut into the shape of a cloud. The blue silk cloud is lightly padded with kapok stuffing.

On both the Spring and Winter pages, the roofs of the houses are built with appliqué. I completed the appliqué first and then filled it with small straight stitches at a later date.

Tip: If you plan to add very delicate fabrics to your work, always do this at a later stage or in the final phase of your making. Delicate fabrics or fine lace can easily be damaged if they're added early in the process.

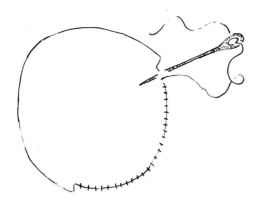

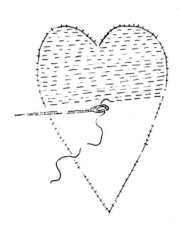

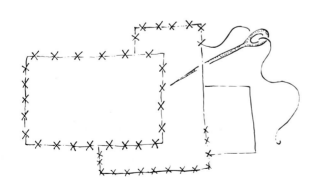

Doodle cloths

I am a huge fan of practising stitches and appliqué techniques. I do this regularly as part of my life as a maker. I would encourage you to practise the stitches and techniques in this book before you start your final version of the project.

The best way to practise stitches is to use a scrap of fabric to experiment on. I have various ongoing doodling cloths both at home and in my studio. Just enjoy playing at this early stage. Place different fabrics together and stitch in and around them with a selection of threads and different stitches – this is a great way to get initial inspiration. Doodle and experiment like this until you feel confident to work into your premade fabric journal. You never know, your doodle cloth could also turn into something beautiful! You can keep your doodle cloths and any notes in your sketchbook. Or hang them up at home for inspiration.

Motifs and transfers

This project revolves around four distinctive artworks that celebrate the seasons: Spring, Summer, Autumn and Winter. The designs are included in the back of the book as transfers that you can use for your own journal.

In addition to the seasonal transfers, there are four additional designs: Heart and Bow (for the front cover); Heart and Dove (for the inside front cover); Pin Cushion (for the inside back cover) and Rosette (for the back cover).

There is also a large selection of smaller, additional templates for you to copy or trace and use in a freestyle manner throughout the project. Because the small designs are not transfers, you will need to trace them to transfer them onto your fabric. Enjoy choosing and embellishing these little designs in your personal making journey. I added the key, butterfly and swan motifs to my journal's front cover. The teacup became part of my inside front cover. The scissor motif is stitched into my journal's inside back cover design, and the coffee pot and bouquet of flowers are very much part of my back cover page design.

Using the small templates

I hand traced and transferred (using tracing paper and a graphite pencil) a selection of these smaller designs onto the same cotton fabric that my journal is made from at the start of my making journey. These small designs are good to use in between the big decisions about embellishing the main seasonal designs. When hand tracing designs with a pencil, consider which way around you want your design to appear on your fabric. You might need to consider mirroring your drawing, if tracing them directly from the small templates in this book.

I mainly filled my small designs with satin stitch and enjoyed adding tiny appliqué details. The butterfly's wings have small, ruched appliqué details, as do the centres of the flowers in the Bouquet design. The teacup has small appliqué detail in the cup's main body and a tiny snippet of doll's dress cuff became the decorative bottom edge to the teacup. The festive bell has a tiny

piece of red checked fabric appliquéd down with the edges tucked under in the middle of the bow. The little scissors are filled with small and irregular satin stitches using one strand each of DMC Mouliné thread in colours 310, 613 and 842.

Incorporating my designs into your journal

Even though you will be using my designs as your main focus throughout this project, it's still important for you to make your own personal version of the project. Each section should be built up using your own personal take on the overall design. To encourage this, many of the designs are either blank in some areas or as simple as possible. This is so that you can customize and personalize each design.

In the Spring motif, the house has been left blank, as has the space directly to the right of the house. In the Summer motif there is space around the washing line and hanging clothing for you to add details from your own garden. In the Autumn motif, the teapot is empty, waiting for your creativity. And finally, in the Winter motif, the main house design is empty. What will you put inside?

You can fill these intentionally blank spaces with some of the smaller template designs from the back of this book, re-sizing or tracing them as needed, or you can stitch and appliqué your own designs directly into them. The possibilities are endless once you start. Have fun choosing!

When attaching small, embellished designs at any stage, refer to my guidance on 'Attaching completed panels to a premade journal'.

About the transfers

The large transfers in this book are designed to be torn or cut out along the perforated lines and ironed directly onto fabric. If you would like to use the designs again, or want them to be smaller or bigger, photocopy them first and save the copies for another project.

Alternatively, you can trace over the transfers using a light box and tracing paper. Trace using a soft pencil. When it's time to use the design, simply rub your traced pencil lines onto your base fabric, before filling the rubbed-off drawings with stitches. This is a simple way to reproduce any drawing or image, at any time. If you don't have a light box, use a window – or the light from a suitable digital device like a tablet or large smartphone works very well.

You can also download the motifs from www.bookmarkedhub.com. The digital files can be printed to any size that you want.

Using the transfers

The transfers at the back of this book are designed to be attached with heat from your iron straight onto your premade fabric journal. Or, alternatively, you could transfer the designs onto a separate piece of fabric and then appliqué the fabric into your journal at a later date. Either way will work.

Be organized, calm and tidy when using the transfers. The transfers are not designed to last for a long time and they cannot be washed, so be mindful of this and only transfer the designs close to the time that you plan to start embellishing them. Once your transfer is fixed there is no going back. Before you start, it's very important to make sure that your base fabric is flat and has been well pressed with your iron. Make sure your transfer is the right way up and is not on a slant when you place it on your fabric.

Step one: Once you are ready and have chosen the position of your motif on your base fabric, tear or cut out your selected design from the back of this book. Trim around your transfer, leaving an edge of white paper roughly 1cm (⅜in) wide.

Step two: Place your transfer, ink-side down onto the base fabric and use pins to secure the transfer to the fabric. With your iron set to a medium-hot heat, press carefully on the back of the transfer paper. Make sure your iron is not too hot, you don't want to accidentally burn your base fabric.

Step three: Take your time and take a peek at the transfer early on in the process. The image will immediately start to transfer onto your base fabric.

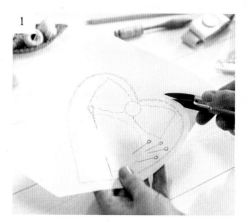

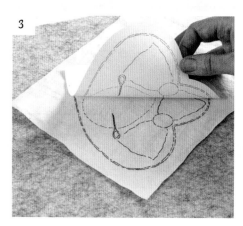

Design your own simple motifs

Take inspiration from the everyday items that surround you at home, and draw directly from them. Create some simple line drawings and then try filling them with stitches. Keep your drawings simple and not too busy; busier drawings are harder to fill with stitches. Play on your doodle cloth first! You can draw directly onto your base fabric or try creating simple motifs using tracing paper and a graphite pencil. Trace directly over a photograph or child's drawing and then rub the design onto your fabrics. Small personal motifs can certainly be combined with the main designs from this book at any stage.

Building a design library

Be sure to keep all your odd, messy tracing bits and bobs safe, even if papers are dirty with pencil marks from your working process. Odd tracing paper scraps with drawings on will become precious and be useful for future projects. Build your own design library! Keep these precious designs safe in your sketchbook or in a box for future inspiration. Also, remember to keep your used transfers from the back of this book. You can trace over them again for use in future projects.

Transfer and template sizes

The dimensions below refer to the transfers and templates at the back of this book. I have included these measurements so that you can follow the sizes exactly if you are planning on tracing the designs at any stage. These measurements are the correct sizes if you are following my guidelines and planning on making your journal 20 x 20cm (8 x 8in).

Please note, I have not provided measurements for the alphabet and number templates. This is simply because I have not used them in my version of the project. Enjoy using them in your journal however you like: trace the designs, scan them, make them larger, make them smaller, or use them at the size they are in the book. It's up to you!

- Heart and Bow (front cover): 14cm (5½in) wide
- Heart and Dove (inside front cover): 13cm (5⅛in) wide
- Spring page: 17cm (6¾in) wide
- Summer page: 17cm (6¾in) wide
- Autumn page: 17cm (6¾in) wide
- Winter page: 17cm (6¾in) wide
- Pin Cushion (inside back cover): 12.5cm (4⅞in) wide
- Rosette (back cover): 10cm (4in) wide
- All additional templates: 6, 7 or 8cm (2⅜, 2¾ or 3⅛in) at their widest points.

Stitch guides

This section of the book celebrates my favourite and most regularly used embroidery stitches and techniques. Bear in mind that these stitches and techniques can vary hugely in style and look when worked in different thread types, thicknesses and weights.

Straight stitch

This is one of the simplest and most versatile freestyle embroidery stitches. It is the stitch I use for securing appliqué shapes, motifs and patches in a decorative style. It is also the stitch I use for attaching completed panels to my premade journal.

For best results, keep your straight stitches small and close together. Try mixing different coloured threads and working the stitches in a variety of slightly different lengths. This might give you an interesting border to an appliquéd shape, or to one of your seasonal panels or cover designs. Straight stitch works well with any thickness of thread, but for best results, work it with one or two strands of DMC Mouliné thread or use DMC Coton Perlé thread.

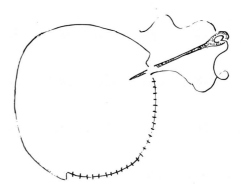

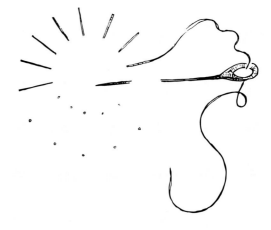

Running stitch

This is a very simple stitch. It is perfect for adding decorative detail or for mending and darning worn fabric. Keep your stitches small and close together, interlacing them with the weave of your base fabric. Be creative by using a variety of different coloured threads and by running your stitches in a variety of different directions.

I enjoy using running stitch to add all sorts of detail to embroidered and appliquéd stories. It is perfect for creating a sky filled with clouds, and a sun or moon can be created in running stitch by stitching in a circle, starting from the outside and working inwards. Running stitch works well when using thinner threads. For best results, work with one or two strands of DMC Mouliné thread or use DMC Coton Perlé thread. Running stitch was used to create the red flower petals on the inside cover of my journal. The sun's rays are represented by yellow running stitches in an abstract square on my Spring page.

Satin stitch

Satin stitch consists of simple straight stitches, packed closely together to fill in an area of a design. When densely worked, it will also give you a beautiful raised effect. It is one of the slower stitches, it takes both time and patience to achieve a smooth, raised surface with neat edges.

Enjoy experimenting with a mixture of different coloured threads to give your work subtle tones and shading. A top tip is never to use different thread thicknesses for satin stitch, as this tends to make your work messy and easy to snag. For best results, work with one or two strands of DMC Mouliné thread or use DMC Coton Perlé thread.

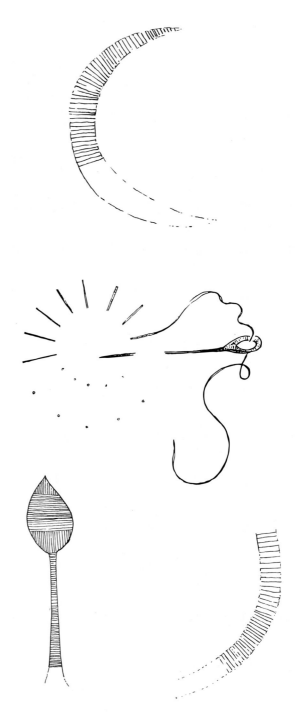

Cross stitch

This is a quick and fun-to-use stitch, ideal for building up
areas and for adding shading. It is perfect for creating a sky
or river, or for filling in the leaves on trees. I regularly use two
different thread colours for cross stitch to achieve a lovely mixed
colourway. You might enjoy using two different tones of green
for shading the greenery of a tree. Or you could combine a
blue thread with a silver thread to fill in clouds, or give the
impression of movement in a sky.

I also use cross stitch as a decorative way of securing needle- or
finger-turned appliqué motifs, shapes and patches. You could
experiment by stitching flowing cross stitches over previously
patched areas to give a scattered effect, or make them in a variety
of different sizes to add textural detail. For the neatest of results,
work with one or two strands of DMC Mouliné thread or use
DMC Coton Perlé thread.

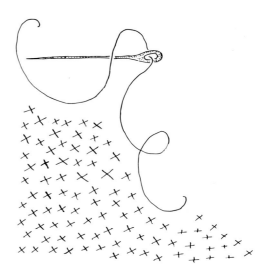

Seed stitch

This stitch involves using small raised stitches to create a random, scattered decorative effect. This allows you to fill in areas quickly. It is one of my go-to stitches for shading. To create perfect raised stitches, use small stabbing stitches on top of one another. Run these stabbing stitches through your fabric two to three times to build up a sufficiently raised stitch.

Experiment with different colours when using this stitch. For best results, avoid using your thinnest threads. This stitch works beautifully with DMC Coton Perlé thread or even with fine crochet cottons.

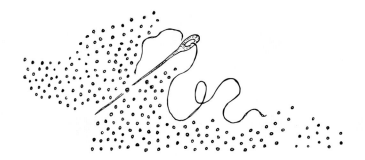

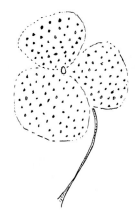

Long seed stitch

Long seed stitch is used to create a random, decorative scattered effect by mixing simple straight stitches of slightly different lengths, worked in a variety of directions. It is a relatively fast stitch, so you can build up areas quickly. My signature style is to use long seed stitch in a variety of different thread colours and stitch sizes when shading large areas of artworks. It is my go-to stitch for shading a sky, a river or a path in a garden scene. The grass on my Summer page in this project was built up with this stitch type.

Enjoy experimenting with different colours – this stitch works beautifully with pearl embroidery threads or even with fine crochet cottons. For best results, work with one or two strands of DMC Mouliné thread or use DMC Coton Perlé thread.

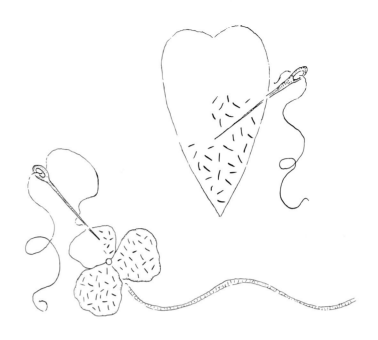

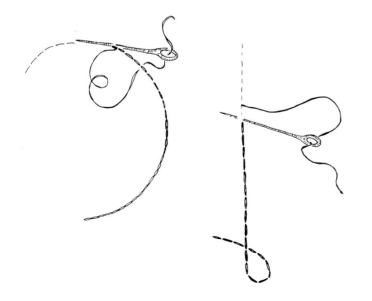

Back stitch

This stitch is ideal for creating neat, linear words, names, dates and motifs. You need to keep your stitches small and close together – with no fabric showing between them – to create a flowing line. Try combinations of different coloured thread; this works very well for lettering and dates.

Back stitch can also be used for creating very strong hems when finishing off projects. I suggest working with one strand of DMC Mouliné thread or use DMC Coton Perlé thread.

Couched work

You will see couched work a lot in my artwork. It is a bold technique, so it stands out. I use it for crafting stand-alone shapes, such as the outline of a house or a tree, or perhaps the sturdy outline of a boat, and I also use it for lettering. It can sometimes be mistaken for dense satin stitch, if your base thread and top thread are the same thickness and colour. Couched work can be done using a wide range of different thread types and thicknesses.

My top tip is to attach your base thread to your ground/base fabric first. To do this, you simply lay down long running stitches, very close together, to outline the shape of your choice, such as a heart, a house or maybe the sun. Then you whip back over this pre-laid base with a top thread using small straight stitches. Couching works best if the thread used for the base is slightly thicker than your top thread. For the most exciting and adventurous results, use a mix of two different coloured threads. Try using a ruby red as your base thread and then whip over it with soft white, or even gold thread. You will get an excellent speckled effect when combining these colours.

For best results when starting out, work with DMC Coton Perlé thread for your base and work back over it with one or two strands of DMC Mouliné thread.

Darning, mending and strengthening fabric

The goal of this peaceful and mindful process is to create a pleasing woven effect, which also strengthens your fabric, when mending holes and worn areas.

Running stitch is my first choice of stitch for darning, mending and strengthening fabric. When mending beloved items as a child by my mum's side, we always used running stitch. This is because of its simplicity.

You can 'walk' your thread in a mixture of different directions. Try to keep your stitches small and close together, interlacing them with the weave of your fabric. The best tip I can give you for darning and mending is to use thread that is a similar thickness to that of the fabric you are working on. This helps with the overall neatness of your final work.

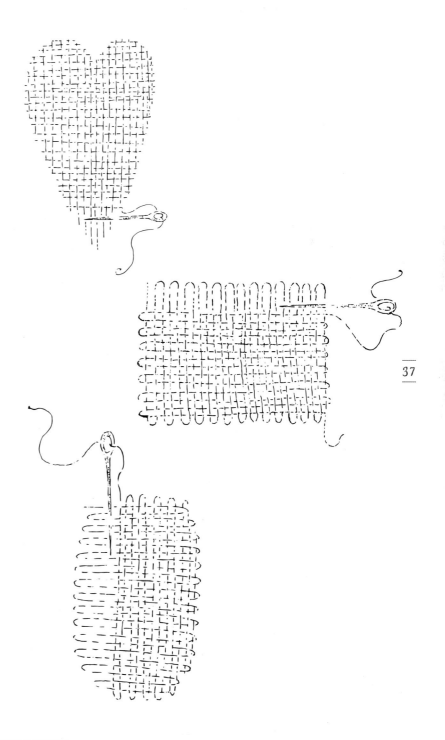

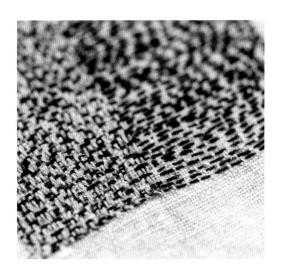

Things to consider

Before you get started, take some time to think about your journal in terms of construction, order of work, colour and purpose.

The making process

Before you start stitching, you need to decide whether to construct your fabric journal as the first stage of this project, meaning the embellishment is carried out on the fully constructed book, or whether to create your pages as separate flat sections and put them together into a fabric journal form later on. In the coming pages, I will explain how to construct first and embellish once your book is complete, because that's the way I tend to work, but either way will work, there are no rules!

You will also need to decide whether or not you want to work through your premade book in a linear fashion, from season to season. The approach I would suggest is to work on the front cover, inside front cover, inside back cover and back cover first to warm up. And then, when spring arrives start on the first of your four seasonal pages with the others following over the months ahead. This approach will also help to make the work free and intuitive. But there are no hard and fast rules, work in whatever fashion makes you feel happy and excited!

Colour continuity

When designing your journal, one thing to consider is colour continuity. In my version of this project, I have used one strand of red and one strand of pink DMC Mouliné thread (colours 321 and 224) together in a number of places throughout the book to give a sense of continuity. Working with both colour threads threaded through the needle produces a flecked and variegated stitch effect, and I have built up satin stitch using these two colours for the main heart on the front cover, for the bow on the back cover and on the top edge of the pin cushion inside the back cover design.

In a similar way, on the four seasonal pages, I have filled both the crosses and the sash/ribbons on the borders with the same colour combination of one strand each of DMC Mouliné thread in colours 407 and 613. This gives a beautiful consistency to all four seasonal page designs. Additionally, throughout my journal, I have used pieces of fine lace in a subtle pinky-brown tone in a variety of different locations. It first appears on the top edge of the front cover but it is also part of the inside front cover, the Winter page, and the inside back cover design.

Who is it for?

Next, and most importantly, you need to consider who you are making this beautiful, slow stitched, seasonal journal for. Is it intended for you? Or is it going to be made with, or for, a family member? Or for a friend? This project is great to make with a child or grandchild, or with a beloved friend or family member. Or is it being made as a gift for a beloved friend to mark an important date? These are all key questions you need to address early on in your design process. They are also important questions to think about before you go about sourcing creative inspiration as well as fabric and threads.

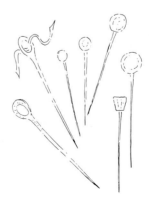

How to make your fabric journal

Constructing your fabric journal

I like to construct my fabric journals first, before I add any embellishments. In this completed state, a soft, padded journal is easy to carry around with you, so it can be taken out and about on your travels, during your four-season making journey. A slightly padded, premade book is a pleasure to work into with needle, thread and fabric.

The fabric journal that I will be guiding you to make in the pages ahead measures 20 x 20cm (8 x 8in). This size has been chosen for the purposes of this book, but you can make your own version of this journal project to any size or shape that you wish. There is also no reason why you can't add more pages. The four seasonal designs could evolve into larger artworks. Your version of this project could flow in all creative directions – you could even make your work into a small memory quilt. The choice is yours!

NOTE: If the method shown here is not your preferred way of working, I suggest you work the instructions back to front. Decorate your seasonal pages and fabric covers in their flat state first, and then construct your fabric journal as the final stage. The order of work is a matter of personal preference; either way works. Just have fun!

Selecting and preparing your base fabric

What are you going to construct your fabric journal from? This is the first decision to make when starting this project. As you will know by now, I strongly encourage using preloved fabrics. A cherished piece of vintage linen, cotton tablecloths, tray cloths, hankies and napkins are all perfect base materials.

Stick with plain fabrics, so that your beautiful stitches will be visible and not lost in a busy pattern, and opt for items made solely from natural fibres, such as cotton or linen, which are easier to work with and will have the weight to hold your highly embellished page designs.

When you're choosing a base fabric, consider deconstructing an existing item. For example, you might find some cotton or linen homeware with a decorative edging. Could you incorporate this detail into your design? Or maybe part of it could become the sash for tying your journal together?

Take care to select fabric that can be cut to 44 x 44cm (17¼ x 17¼in), so that it will be large enough to make a 20 x 20cm (8 x 8in) journal.

Always clean and wash base fabrics before cutting and construction. Preloved and found fabrics will likely have been washed many times in their life, and they should not shrink, but make sure by washing and ironing fabrics in advance.

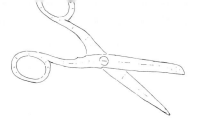

My journal

To make my version of this seasonal, stitched journal, I used one large cotton kitchen towel. When I found this fabric towel at a market in East London, I was told that it had come from an old house in rural France and would have originally been used for drying glass in the family home. My entire journal is constructed from this one cotton panel. And I used another identical cotton panel, on which I traced some of the smaller template designs, before filling them in.

However, you do not have to use just one fabric for your journal construction, you could easily stitch different fabrics of a similar weight together to make your journal.

If your chosen base fabric is worn and needs mending, refer to the 'Darning, mending and strengthening fabric' techniques. Signs of wear and tear can be beautiful – enjoy making them into a feature!

Selecting a filling or padding

Try to use padding that is made from something that has had a previous life. For my journal, I used a piece of vintage wool blanket. It's the perfect thickness for this type of project. Have a rummage in your local thrift shops, visit a market or even have a look at home! Well-worn and washed wool jumpers are also great for this purpose, especially ones that have become felted over time from washing.

NOTE: Take time to consider the weight of the fabric you select. If you are working with heavier fabric then the panel, which will form the inside four pages of your journal, will need to be cut slightly shorter than your outside panel. This is an important consideration when selecting your base fabric and padding. Also, if your fabric is heavy or thick you may need to make your hems a little bigger. These are all personal creative and technical choices to make during the design process of your book's construction.

Before you start

Prepare a clean and well-lit workspace, ideally with a source of natural light. Gather your favourite tools and anything else that you may need around you, and have your iron and ironing board or felt ironing mat close to hand.

Once your workspace is ready and you have selected, washed and pressed your base fabric and padding, it's time to start constructing the two double-sided and lightly padded panels that will make up the journal. One panel will be folded to create the outside and inside covers, and one will be folded to make the four inner pages. The two panels will both be the same size, measuring exactly 40 x 20cm (15¾ x 8in).

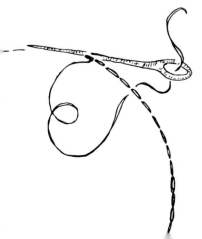

NOTE: I suggest making a simple paper or cotton fabric pattern for the panels, to help you understand the sizes that you need to cut your base fabric and padding to. This will help a lot and will prevent any mistakes. I often make rough patterns like this from large sheets of tracing paper, or from thin cotton fabric, cutting and folding and double checking my measurements until I am happy to start constructing using my precious base fabric.

Step one: Cutting your base fabric

You will need to cut your main base fabric slightly bigger than the final panel sizes. Cut the two pieces of base fabric to exactly 44 x 44cm (17¼ x 17¼in) – one for each of the double-sided panels. This sizing allows for a reasonably wide hem to tuck under before padding and stitching.

Step two: Folding the base fabric

Fold both pieces of base fabric in half. Each should now measure 44 x 22cm (17¼ x 8¾in). Carefully press them with your iron.

Step three: Cut the padding to size

Measure and cut your two pieces of padding to the size the two panels will be once stitched and hemmed: 40 x 20cm (15¾ x 8in).

Step four: Padding the journal

Press the padding with the iron and sandwich each one between the two pieces of cotton base fabric. Tuck the raw edges of your base fabric around the padding and secure with long metal pins. Finally, press the three tucked under edges carefully with the iron and take a moment to check that both panels are even and the same size. However, a little wobble here and there can be charming. How neat and straight you want your fabric journal to be depends on you!

NOTE: If needed, at this stage shorten one of your panels slightly, so that it tucks inside the outer panel (the cover). Do this by pulling back the base fabric and trimming the padding slightly. You will only need to cut a small amount off. Do this slowly and carefully, adjusting both panels as you feel necessary, until they fit snugly together.

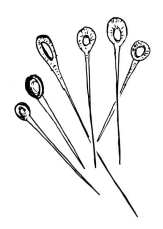

1

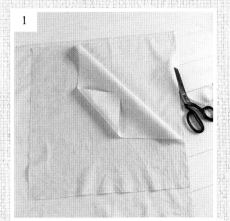

2

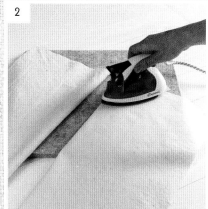

3

4

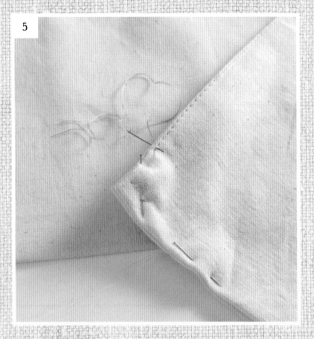

Step five: Stitching the fabric panels

For best results, I suggest using two stands of DMC Mouliné thread, or alternatively DMC Coton Perlé thread (in No. 8 thickness), for stitching the panels closed.

Tie a knot at the end of your thread, and hide it in the turned under base fabric edge. Do the same each time you renew the thread. To fasten off your thread, hide it in the hem. If knots happen to appear on the panels, don't worry! You can cover them with a small patch of fabric at a later date.

Stitch all the way around the four edges of the two fabric panels, not just the three tucked-under edges. Use either small straight stitches or small, stabbing running stitches, which go through both sides of your panel. You could try experimenting by sewing different stitch styles all around your panel edges. This would be fun and would make your journal covers very decorative, like a stitch sampler.

Tip: Keep small snips or scissors to hand while sewing your panels up and trim off any unwanted thicker bits of fabric at the corners as you go. This will help when pushing the needle through bulky edges and hems.

I used small, stabbing running stitches, using two strands of DMC Mouliné thread in colour 842. I used this muted, neutral tone so that my journal would not have a brightly stitched thick edge to it. Using more than one colour around the edges of your panels is also an option.

Once your edges are complete, press both of the stitched-up double-sided panels.

Step six: Folding and binding the journal

Fold both padded panels in half separately, pressing again on both sides, so that you create a crease and a spine (this will help to guide you when you are stitching and binding the panels together)

Place one panel inside the other. If you have made one panel slightly bigger than the other, make sure the bigger one becomes your journal's cover. The smaller panel will now sit snugly inside the bigger panel. If needed, temporarily hold your panels together with a few pins.

Take a long, sharp needle and an arm's length of DMC Coton Perlé thread (I used colour 321) and, working from the outside panel, push your needle into the folded spine on the outside of the book. Push the needle and thread through the folded spine of both panels, and then bring your needle and thread back through from the inside of your spine approximately 10cm (4in) from the first needle hole, so that the thread meets its tail. Once you have made this big stitch through both panels, run the thread through the same needle holes for a second time to really secure the binding stitch. Tie the thread in a big double knot to secure. At this point you can also add a button if you wish. The button is purely for decoration. Adding decorative details like this early on can be really encouraging.

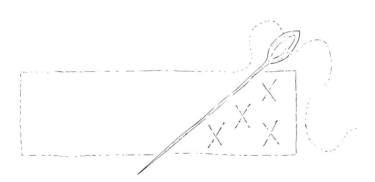

Suffolk puffs or yoyos

Suffolk puffs, or yoyos, are circles of fabric that are gathered in to make them puffy. I collect beautiful vintage Suffolk puffs, like the dusky pink one used here. You can buy them in thrift stores and markets. Or, you could try making your own from a circle of fabric. Thinner fabrics work best. There are lots of online tutorials available and some craft suppliers even sell yoyo-making tools.

Before attaching the Suffolk puff/ yoyo, work into the edge of the fabric puff with small straight stitches. I used one strand of DMC Mouliné thread in each of three colours: 321, 407 and 842.

47

Fastenings

There are so many ways one can create a fastening for a stitched journal. I am a huge fan of constructing ties and fastenings by stitching strips of fabric together with their edges tucked under; however, a piece of ribbon or lace will work just as well. Words and dates can also be stitched into sashes and ties.

Take inspiration from your personal collection and fabric stash and see what jumps out at you. You may have the perfect piece of lace or velvet ribbon waiting.

You might want to experiment with different fastening styles – for instance, you could try using a button fastening as an alternative. I make my fabric books over a period of days, months and often years, and I often take them with me when I travel. Therefore I prefer a tie fastening, which can act as a safety harness while working on my books.

Step seven: Adding a sash

Making a fastening or sash for your journal can be done at any stage, but in this case, we are adding it early on so that it is part of the journal's overall design.

For my journal, I created a fastening from a length of beautiful old cotton tape, which I cut in half to create two ties. I stitched one half of the tape to the edge of the journal's front cover (**7a**). I placed a dusky pink vintage Suffolk puff/yoyo on top of my fabric tape, and on top of this I placed a worn linen button (**7b**). The button is decorative but also helps secure everything in place. The Suffolk puff/yoyo is purely for decoration.

Using DMC Coton Perlé thread in colour 321, I made one big red stitch, straight down though the linen button, Suffolk puff/yoyo, fabric tape and book cover, and then reversed this stitch from inside the cover, coming back out through the button. To secure everything I knotted both ends of the thread together twice and cut the ends neatly, but not too short (**7c**). I then stitched the other piece of tape to the edge of the journal's back cover and added a button at the same time.

Step eight: Starting to fill your journal

Once you have completed the construction stages, you can enjoy starting to fill your journal with your own unique take on this seasonal project. Incorporate favourite decorative stitch techniques, as well as decorative appliqué details. Take inspiration from the stitch guide and the guides to appliqué and darning. Even treasured paper items can be secured in place with a stitch or two, or with a pin. If you wish to include paper items in your work, my advice is to do this at a late stage of making your journal, as paper items are not as durable as fabric. To stitch paper items to fabrics use a very sharp and thin needle. Don't use glue!

My best advice is: don't rush the next stages of this project. Take time to live with your beautifully constructed fabric journal while you gather inspiration and materials.

Also take time to decide if you will be transferring your motifs from the back of this book directly onto your pages, or if you will transfer them onto separate fabrics first and then stitch them into your book at a later date.

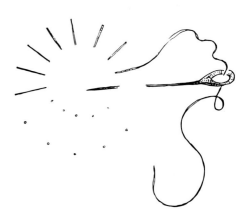

7a

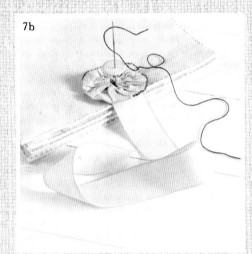

7b

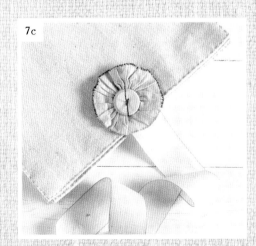

7c

8

Attaching completed panels to a premade journal

At this stage you could embroider and appliqué directly onto the pages of your premade journal or you could work on the page designs separately and stitch them into the journal when they're finished.

For my own journal, I worked on the eight designs first, fully embellishing them, and even adding objects and appliqué details. Then I appliquéd the eight embroidered panels into my premade fabric journal.

Step one: Trimming the panel
To attach your completed panels to the fabric journal, first trim back the edges of each embroidered design, leaving roughly 1cm (⅜in) to tuck under and stitch down. My fabric was originally a lot larger than needed, but it's helpful to work on a larger piece of fabric initially and cut it back later.

Step two: Pressing and pinning
Next, place the panels on the fabric journal and secure in place with pins. Work with your iron and the positioning of the pins until the panel is neat and correctly positioned.

Step three: Stitching
Stitch all the way around each decorative design using small straight stitches. However, don't stitch through all the fabric layers, only the uppermost fabric. This way your stitches won't show through on the other side of your fabric page. Repeat this technique for all sections of the journal. I used different thread colours, but always in muted and light colours when attaching my decorative panels. I chose lighter tones so they did not take away focus from my eight highly embellished designs.

Step four: Using stuffing or wadding (batting)
For the Heart and Bow (front cover) and Pin Cushion (inside back cover) designs I used kapok stuffing to add padding. To do this, leave a small gap when stitching the panels down and use the gap to add stuffing. Continue stitching around the panels until they are completely stitched down. To give them a nice finished look, press the two stuffed panels with a warm iron.

Step five: Adding appliquéd details
Finally, I added small, scattered appliquéd details. This is a nice way to finish any of the page and cover designs in your journal. Small areas of appliqué can bring an entire design together into a state of completeness. Don't be afraid to leave some areas a little unfinished with space to breathe. You can come back at the end of your making journey and add appliqué details, the odd decorative stitch, or an assortment of the smaller template designs from the back of this book. To attach pre-embellished small template designs, work in the same way as for attaching the main panels to the journal.

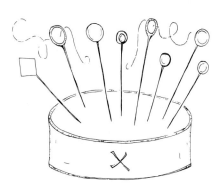

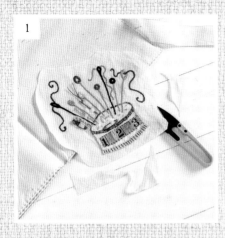

1

4

2

5

3

Front cover

This motif, titled Heart and Bow, features a blank inner area, which is the perfect place for your journal's title. You could also stitch a name or date here. For my own front cover design, I added a yellow, vintage fabric flower with a net bow and satin-stitched stem to this area. This design also incorporates couching, seed stitch and running stitch, and the three additional smaller motifs are appliquéd onto the cover.

Front cover design

Think of your front cover as the door that leads the viewer into the embroidered world that you have created. How will you make the front cover design personal to your seasonal story? What will you add? Really take time over your front cover. Make it a statement piece that you are proud of.

NOTE: By now you should have attached your front cover transfer design to your base fabric. For tips, tricks and inspiration refer back to 'Using the transfers'.

Initially, I worked into the main border of the heart, building up the shape with satin stitch using DMC Mouliné thread (**1**). I combined one strand of red and one of pink (colours 321 and 224) together in the needle to create a variegated stitch.

Next, I couched down a double line of thin vintage gold thread around the outer line of the bow (**2**). Think about what you could couch around the bow and test a few techniques out on your doodle cloth. The bow is filled with fine lines of small running stitches, worked in one strand of DMC Mouliné thread in colour 842 (**3**).

To build up the inner blank space that displays the yellow flower, I stitched small, irregular satin stitches around the border using one strand each of DMC Mouliné thread in colours 730, 3852 and 613 (**4**).

To embellish the large needle and pins motifs, I used one strand each of DMC Mouliné thread in colours 648 and 310. I also used a variety of vintage threads to add colour to the tips of the pins (**5**). Try doing the same on your own design. Add precious threads from your own collection to create pops of colour. Tiny running stitches represent the thread in the large needle (**6**). For these little stitches I used one strand of DMC Mouliné thread in colour 321.

To embellish the inner heart, I stitched a scattering of small, straight seed stitches (**4, 6**) using one strand of DMC Mouliné thread in colour 613, and then added a vintage enamel clock face to the centre of the bow (**7**). I fixed this in place with a small

pearl button using DMC Coton Perlé thread in colour 321 as I wanted it to match the red stitching used in the construction of the journal. In the central space, I added a yellow, vintage fabric flower, with a net bow tied around its stem (**4**). The stem of the flower was made using small, irregular satin stitches using one strand of DMC Mouliné thread in colour 890. This same thread was used to create the small, scattered straight stitches around the flower's head. At the tip of the stem is a splash of light pink vintage thread, worked in satin stitch.

For tips on how I finished this page and how I went about padding the completed design, please refer back to 'Attaching completed panels to a premade journal'.

Extra embellishments

Once I had finished working on the main heart motif, and after the panel had been stitched onto my fabric book, I went back and added some extra embellishments.

I added three of the small templates from the back of this book: the key, the swan and the butterfly. These were all embellished first and then appliquéd to the front cover at a later stage. I also added a scattering of appliquéd patches and cross stitches to tie everything together. I stitched a flower just under the key: this was built up in satin stitch, mainly using vintage threads. The lines that bounce out of the top of the heart are couched using vintage silk threads.

A piece of lace in a subtle pinky-brown tone has been stitched to the top edge of the book cover. Pink running stitches, made from vintage thread, run around the entire border. These same running stitches run around both the front and back covers of my book.

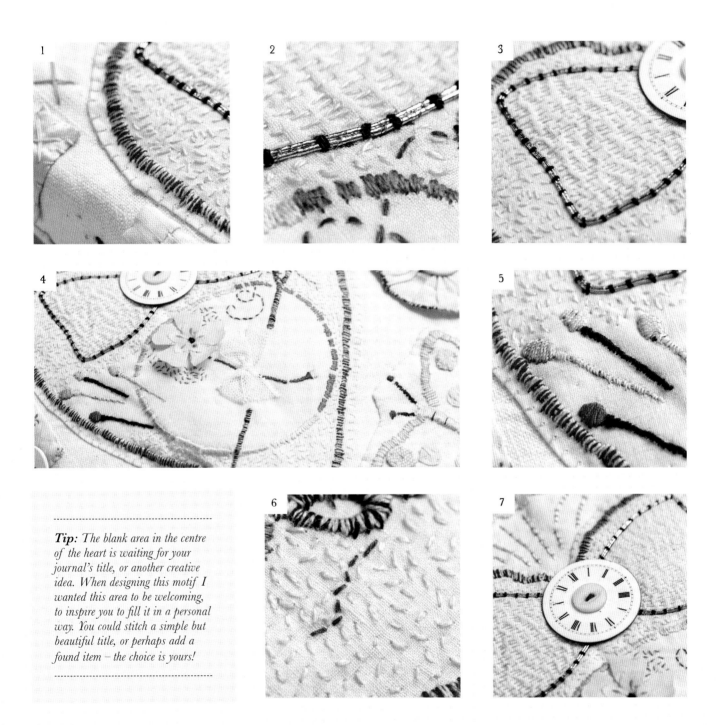

1

2

3

4

5

6

7

Tip: The blank area in the centre of the heart is waiting for your journal's title, or another creative idea. When designing this motif I wanted this area to be welcoming, to inspire you to fill it in a personal way. You could stitch a simple but beautiful title, or perhaps add a found item – the choice is yours!

Inside front cover

This motif, titled Heart and Dove, is mainly stitched in vintage threads and also incorporates a beautiful found fabric flower to tie in with the floral themes on other pages. I added several additional motifs around the central heart design, some appliquéd and others embroidered directly onto the page. The strip of fine lace at the top of the page has continued over from the front cover.

Inside front cover design

How will you make this design personal to your journal? What will you add to build up the dove motif? How will you fill the small heart?

NOTE: By now you should have attached your inside front cover transfer design to your base fabric. For tips, tricks and inspiration refer back to 'Using the transfers'.

First of all, I worked the main heart-shaped border, building up the outline using couching (**1**). As my couching base thread, I used one strand of pink vintage thread. Then, using a vintage black thread, I stitched back over the pink base thread with small straight stitches, to create a raised and speckled effect.

To build up the small heart motif (**2**), I chose vintage pink and blue silk threads that have a beautiful shine to them. I worked these two threads in dense satin stitch. Later, I added small, scattered seed stitches to the inside of the sacred heart using much finer vintage silk thread, this time in blue and dark pink. You could do the same or you could cut a piece of fabric and appliqué the heart area, padding out your appliqué so that it becomes raised. You could then work into the appliqué, adding a date or an initial.

The dove motif was outlined using fine satin stitches, worked in one strand of DMC Mouliné thread in colour 613 (**3**). Later, I went back and added further areas of satin stitch (over the initial satin stitch), again in DMC Mouliné thread, using one strand each of colours 842 and 407.

On the dove's wing, I couched down a piece of rough silver thread, using vintage yellow thread with small straight stitches to hold the silver thread down (**4**). I also added scattered long seed stitches to the dove's tail feathers, using vintage thread (**5**).

The lines that radiate out from the dove were built up in satin stitch using a selection of fine vintage threads in yellow, beige and blue (**6**).

The small lines that run from the smaller heart (**7**) are simply long straight stitches using a combination of one strand each of DMC Mouliné thread in colours 321 and 224.

To complete the design, I added a vintage silk flower to the top of the heart (**8**). I wanted beautiful old flowers to be part of my overall seasonal story, so this would tie into other areas of my journal where vintage flowers are used.

What do you have that you could add to the design? A bow or button would sit beautifully at the top of this heart design. Or even a simple rag bow? You may have some flowers from your wedding day or another memorable event?

Extra embellishments

To further embellish the inside front cover, I added the teacup motif from the back of this book. There is a piece of fine lace stitched to the top left edge of the page. This lace has travelled over from the front cover. The lace is secured with a linen button.

At the top right of the page, I have densely satin stitched a moon, using vintage threads. To the top left, I have stitched a sun. The sun is mainly worked in satin stitch. The centre of the sun was made using one strand of DMC Mouliné thread in colour 3852. The rays of the sun were made using vintage threads. Inside the sun are tiny, raised seed stitches.

On the bottom right is a flower. The petals are small running stitches worked in one strand of DMC Mouliné thread in colour 321. The stem and petals are made in satin stitch, as is the yellow stitch in the centre of the flower. Around the yellow centre of the flower are small black back stitches. The scattering of stitches around the flower are small, straight seed stitches. So that this page was consistent with other pages in my journal, I have added patches of appliquéd fabric detail.

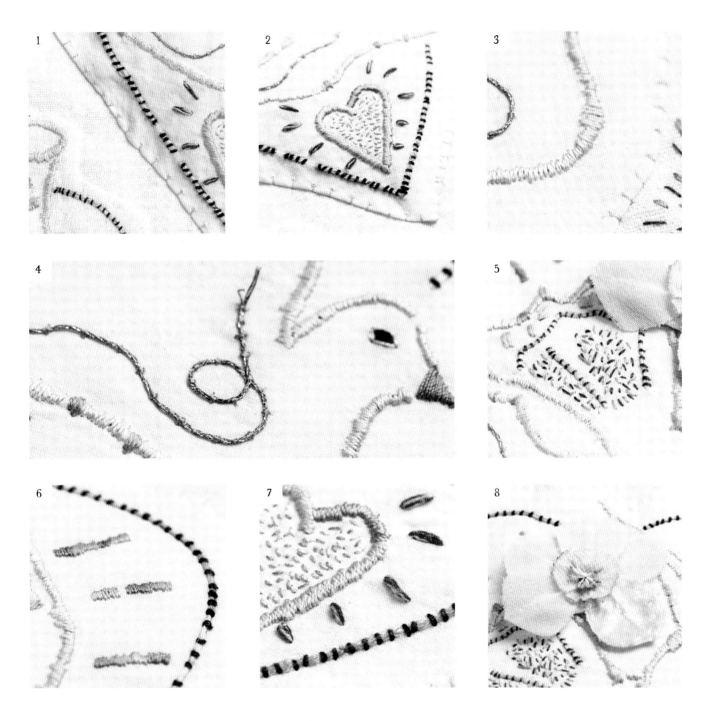

INSIDE FRONT COVER DESIGN

Spring page

Welcome to Spring! This page features a house set in a beautiful garden and basking in spring sunshine. The house roof is a piece of silk fabric appliquéd in place and then filled with small straight stitches to add detail. This page also has several other textural effects: the flowers on the tree are made with snippets of silk fabric, the centre of the sun is a linen button, and the sky is decorated with small glass beads.

Spring page design

Think about how you will make this design personal to you. What will you add to the blank space inside the house? Will you add anything to the space to the right of the house?

NOTE: By now you should have attached your Spring transfer design to your base fabric. For tips, tricks and inspiration refer back to 'Using the transfers'.

Adding appliqué details is a good way to jump in and start a design like this quickly. Consider adding the appliqué as a first stage that will be followed up with further embellishments. I created an appliquéd roof for my house initially, and then went on to fill the roof with small straight stitches at a later date (**1**).

A snippet of silk handkerchief became the blossoms in the tree (**2**). I cut small circles of the silk fabric and attached them with a few little stitches though the centre of the circles, scrunching them up slightly as I stitched them down. I also added tiny glass beads to my thread as I ran the small stitches though the fabric circles.

To build up the tree trunk, I ran satin stitch around it, starting from the top of the design and working right down to the border of the page (**3**). I used DMC Mouliné thread for this, with one strand each of colours 3031 and 613. I worked the two threads separately, stitching with the brown thread first and then filling in the gaps with the white-toned thread.

To create the tree's leafy top, I once again used satin stitch, this time using one strand of DMC Mouliné thread in colour 3362 (**4**).

I attached a linen button to the centre of the sun using a bright orange vintage thread to secure the button (**5**). To create the sun's rays, I stitched fine lines of satin stitch using both vintage orange thread from my own collection and one strand of DMC Mouliné thread in colour 3852 (**5, 6**).

63

To add detail and texture to the sky above the house, I stitched down small white glass beads using a variety of different vintage blue threads for the stitches (**7**). How will you fill this area? You could add silver sequins, a snippet of appliquéd fabric or fine lace could become a cloud?

The rainbow was created by working small irregular, satin stitches using vintage threads (**8**).

The chimneys of the house were built up with satin stitch using one strand of DMC Mouliné thread in colour 407 (**8**). They have black tips worked in satin stitch using one strand of DMC Mouliné thread in colour 310. With this same black thread, I added more satin stitch to the sides of my appliquéd silk roof.

The garden fence was created using one strand of fine jute string as a base, which was secured in place with one strand of DMC Mouliné thread in colour 890 (**9**).

The stems and leaves of the flowers in the garden were mainly built by working small satin stitches using one strand each of DMC Mouliné thread in colours 730 and 890 (**10**). Again, using satin stitch, the petals were stitched in a variety of vintage threads. The dots in the centre of the flowers are raised seed stitches in vintage thread. You could also add little beads into the inner areas of the flowers, or tiny buttons.

On the blank area to the right of the house I placed a vintage silk flower (**11**). The paper-wrapped wire stem of this flower is couched down using one strand of DMC Mouliné thread in colour 890. The couched wire stem continues to grow out and away from the Spring embroidery panel and onto the journal's base page (**12**). The positioning of the flower, and the stem in particular, is intended to evoke a feeling of growth, hope and new beginnings, the feeling one gets when the spring season is approaching

The main shape of the house is built in satin stitch using one strand of DMC Mouliné thread in colour 842 (**13**).

To complete the Spring page, I added one of my favourite motifs, something that is personal to my own artwork: a little chair, sitting on a rug in the centre of the main house design (**13**). What will you add to the inner blank space of the house design?

Extra embellishments

The appliquéd cotton fabric patches on this page continue over on to my Summer page. The patches are cut from a section of vintage patchwork quilt, which I treasure and use sparingly. To the top right-hand side of this page, I have stitched a flower. This flower is mainly worked in satin stitch using vintage threads. The leaf is made from three lines of very small running stitch in a vintage green thread.

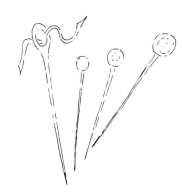

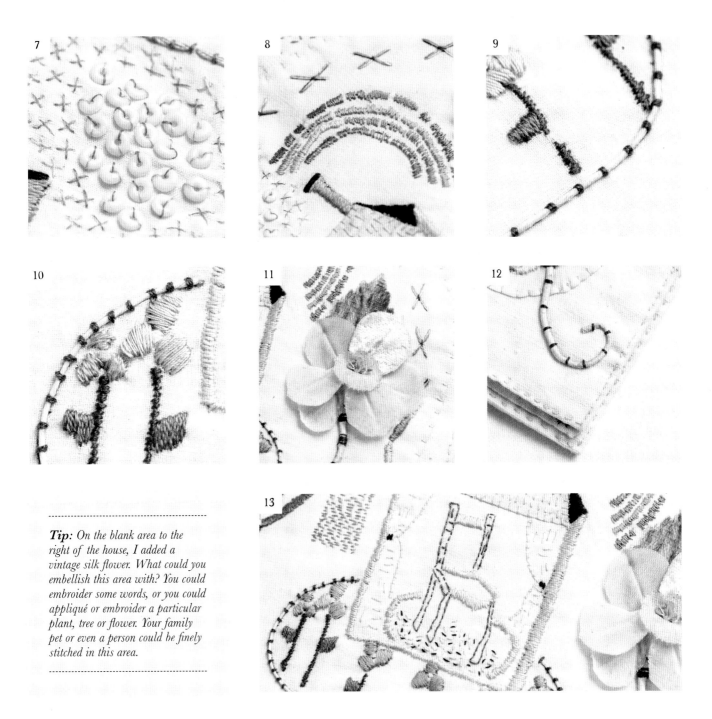

65

Tip: *On the blank area to the right of the house, I added a vintage silk flower. What could you embellish this area with? You could embroider some words, or you could appliqué or embroider a particular plant, tree or flower. Your family pet or even a person could be finely stitched in this area.*

SPRING PAGE DESIGN

Summer page

We've arrived in Summer! The design for this page features a washing line full of freshly laundered clothes drying in a sunny garden. Much of the embroidery is worked in satin stitch, often using two colours together for a variegated effect. A Suffolk puff/yoyo is held in place with small white beads, stitched on with blue vintage thread, while seed stitches are used to create the effect of sunlight and to secure the scrunched up fabric that creates the appliquéd lawn.

Summer page design

Think about how you can make this washday design personal to your story.
What will you add to the blank spaces above and below the washing line?

NOTE: By now you should have attached your Summer transfer design to your base fabric. For tips, tricks and inspiration refer back to 'Using the transfers'.

To outline the hanging clothes, I used a fine satin stitch, mainly using one strand each of DMC Mouliné thread in colours 613 and 842 (**1**). These threads were worked separately and not combined together. The colourful splashes on the clothes were built in satin stitch in a variety of mainly vintage threads. I wanted the washing to be white in tone with dashes of colour.

The washing line itself was created in satin stitch using one strand of DMC Mouliné thread in colour 648 (**2**).

To build up the tree trunk, I ran satin stitches around it from top to bottom (**3**). To do this, I used one strand each of DMC Mouliné thread in colours 3031 and 842. The two threads were worked running through my needle together to create the variegated effect.

The tree's leafy summer top is built up in satin stitch, using one strand each of DMC Mouliné thread in colours 890 and 730 (**4**).

The summer blossoms in the tree were created using satin stitch, working with two strands each of DMC Mouliné thread in colours 224 and 842 (**5**).

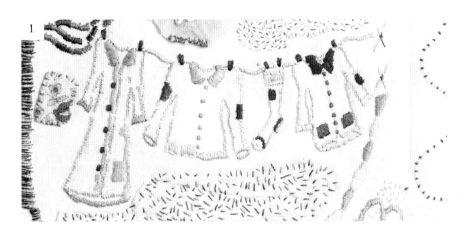

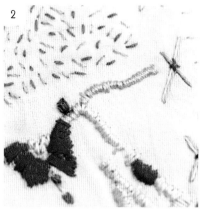

Tip: *Consider using appliqué details to embellish the clothes in this design. This is a great opportunity to use odd fabric scraps; thinner fabrics like cottons and silks. You could use snippets of cloth that remind you of dear friends or a family member.*

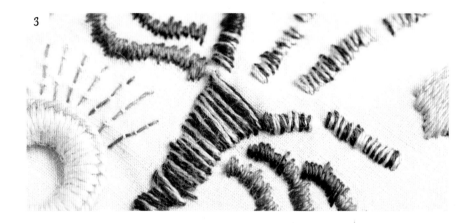

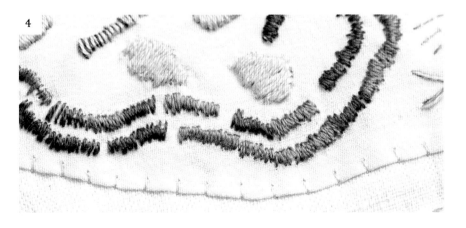

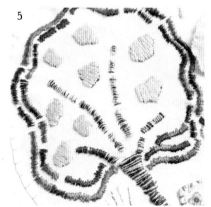

To create the sun, I took a small circle of yellow silk and placed a fine white fabric beneath it (**6**). These fabrics were stitched in place using a few scattered straight seed stitches in yellow and orange vintage threads.

The sun's rays are stitched in fine lines of satin stitch using a gorgeous, vintage rich orange thread, combined with lines of satin stitch using one strand of DMC Mouliné thread in colour 3852. Some of the sun's rays are couched using DMC Coton Perlé thread in colour 3033 (**7, 9**). The Coton Perlé base thread is held in place with small, straight stitches made using a vintage orange thread.

The lines of blue sky/cloud are built using satin stitch, using one strand of vintage thread in two different tones of blue (**8**).

The sun's rays that appear under the sun and above the washing are worked in fine seed stitches – think of them as sunlight (**9**). They are made using one strand of fine vintage thread.

To add detail to the sky above the washing line, I stitched down a small off-white/dirty pink Suffolk puff/yoyo. Small white glass beads and vintage blue thread are used to both add detail and secure the puff in place (**10**). Before attaching the puff, I stitched into its edges with odd-coloured threads. The aim was to add the feeling of a summer sky to this raised area. How will you fill the summer sky? You could fill it with fine, raised seed stitches. Or silver stitches. Or small beads or sequins.

The lawn in the summer garden was created by cutting a piece of fine white fabric and scrunching it up as it was sewn into place to create a wavy, folded effect (**11**). The fabric is stitched down with small, scattered long seed stitches, worked using one strand each of DMC Mouliné thread in colours 890 and 730. These two threads were worked individually through my needle and not twisted together. This gives a busy speckled effect to this area. You could also use lines of running stitch for this grassy area or wiggly lines of irregular satin stitch, or even cross stitch in two shades of green thread.

Extra embellishments

This page already felt very busy and complete, with no need for a lot of further embellishments. The appliquéd cotton fabric patches continue over onto this page from my Spring page and are again snippets from a vintage patchwork quilt. On the top left of this page, I have stitched a circle of running stitches using vintage orange thread. This was to create an abstract sun motif. To complete this Summer page, I embroidered a flower to the bottom right-hand corner. The flower is mainly built in satin stitch using vintage threads. Small straight seed stitches are scattered around the head of the flower in a bright green thread.

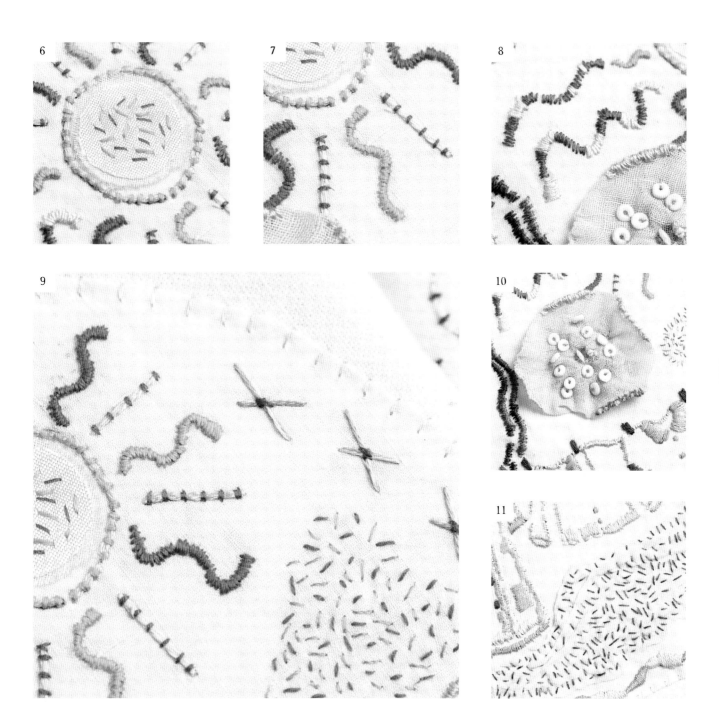

SUMMER PAGE DESIGN

Autumn page

Here comes Autumn! This page features an
oversized teapot, surrounded by an autumn
garden, with one large tree. Appliqué is used for
the cloud, moon and to add pieces of vintage
quilt, while a length of jute string is couched in
a wavy line under the teapot, then is taken down
and over into the following page. I have also used
some precious and found objects on this page:
heart and arrow charms, and a small scrap of
silver card held in place with a tiny pearl button.

Autumn page design

How will you make this cozy teatime scene feel personal to you?
What will you add to the blank space inside the oversized teapot?

NOTE: By now you should have attached your Autumn transfer design to your base fabric. For tips, tricks and inspiration refer back to 'Using the transfers'.

To begin, I created the raised blue appliqué cloud (**1**). It was made using a snippet of fabric cut from an old dress sleeve. This silk cloud is slightly padded using kapok stuffing. I then added fine couched detail and also a little satin stitch to the cloud using vintage threads from my own collection. To the right of the cloud I scattered small cross stitches using vintage threads in blues and a yellow colour.

The appliqué moon motif (**2**) was created from a piece of fine yellow silk, which is stitched down all the way around the outside (the silk is not tucked under, it is raw edged) with a mix of yellow and blue vintage threads. The inside of the moon is filled with straight, long seed stitches, worked using vintage threads.

Two strands of fine jute string are couched to create the grass or lawn effect under the teapot (**4**). The jute string flows off the Autumn design and onto the rest of the journal page (**3**), before continuing over and onto the next page in my journal, which is the Winter page. This represents the changing of the seasons. How could you add similar details to your work?

The base of the teapot was built by couching down a thin strip of very fine grey linen fabric (**4**). Holding it in place are small straight stitches. The linen was first rolled up and the edges tucked under, but note the ends are left raw.

The main body of the teapot is built up in satin stitch (**5, 6**). The brown around the lid (**6**) is also satin stitch made in a fine vintage thread that came from a Belgian flea market. The black and white embroidery (**6**) are single strands of DMC Mouliné thread in colours 310 and 613, again worked in satin stitch.

The teapot's handle (**5**) and spout (**6**) are created from satin stitch, worked using two strands of contrasting thread placed through the needle together. This creates a mottled but very subtle variegated effect. One strand each of DMC Mouliné thread in colours 613 and 224 is used for this. To create the fine black lines I stitched over the teapot's handle and spout one last time with satin stitch using one strand of DMC Mouliné thread in colour 310 (**5, 6**), but just in odd places to give some punch and sharpness to these areas.

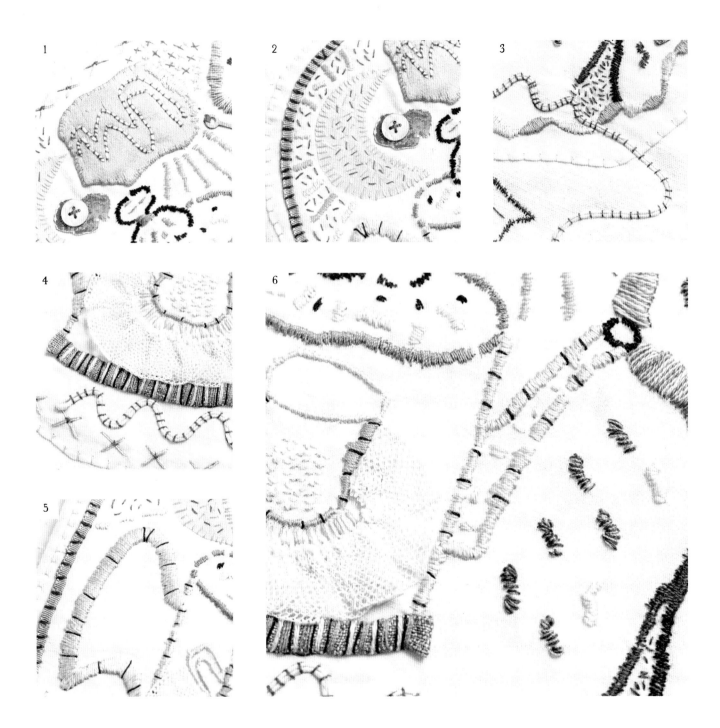

AUTUMN PAGE DESIGN

I have added a teacup motif to the centre of the teapot (**7**). The saucer is made from a piece of vintage net ribbon. The little cup is built up in satin stitch using one strand of DMC Mouliné thread (colour 842) combined with a spool of vintage thread. Tiny seed stitches in these two same threads are scattered in the middle of the cup, and straight stitches are used to create a border or base for the cup.

The left-hand border of this Autumn design was created by couching down a piece of gorgeous, dirty-brown ribbon, which is held in place with thick straight stitches made using two strands of DMC Mouliné thread in colour 890 (**8**).

To fill the Autumn tree trunk, I worked fine satin stitch using one strand of DMC Mouliné thread in colour 3031 (**9**). For the upper branches, I combined the same brown coloured thread with a soft pinky-brown vintage thread, using just one strand of each thread and working them side by side. To fill the inside area at the bottom of the tree trunk, I stitched small, scattered seed stitches using one strand of DMC Mouliné thread in colour 890 (**10**).

To build up the tree's leafy top, I used one strand each of DMC Mouliné thread in colours 3362 and 842. The two threads were worked running through my needle together, as I worked dense satin stitch to create the variegated effect (**9, 10**). In the blank area under the tree there are small areas of satin stitch (**10**). These are intended to look like falling autumn leaves. I wanted to evoke a feeling of coziness, and to remind people of that crackling noise you get when walking on fallen leaves in the autumn, when you're heading home for a nice cup of tea. What might you add to this blank space? You could add some words or a poem. You could also add a person or a family pet?

To add further depth to my Autumn page, I added two metal charms. A heart (**11**) is stitched to the right-hand side of the design and a little metal arrow (**12**) is stitched down next to the rays of autumn sunlight, which are shining out from behind the blue silk cloud. The rays of sunlight were created with satin stitch using one strand of DMC Mouliné thread in colour 3852 combined with a beautiful, fine blue vintage thread.

Finally, and at a much later stage, I added a scrap of silver foil-covered cardboard (originally cut from a card that displayed French linen buttons). This is held in place with a small pearl button (**13**). The scrap of card and button are positioned to enhance the sense of the beautiful and strong sunlight that we experience in early autumn days. It also celebrates my passion for collecting and saving odd but beautiful fragmented items. What paper or card items can you use in a similar fashion in this area?

Extra embellishments

Once I had finished working on the main Autumn motif, I went back and added some extra embellishments. I embroidered two autumn leaves flowing in different directions onto the outside edges of the page. A snippet of soft red fabric from a vintage patchwork quilt is appliquéd to the top right of the page and wraps over the page edge and onto my Winter page. There is also a couched cross stitch on this red patch, made using vintage threads. A long patch of soft, stripy cotton fabric runs over the top edge and again, this becomes part of my Winter page. To add one final detail, I appliquéd another patch of cotton fabric from a vintage patchwork quilt.

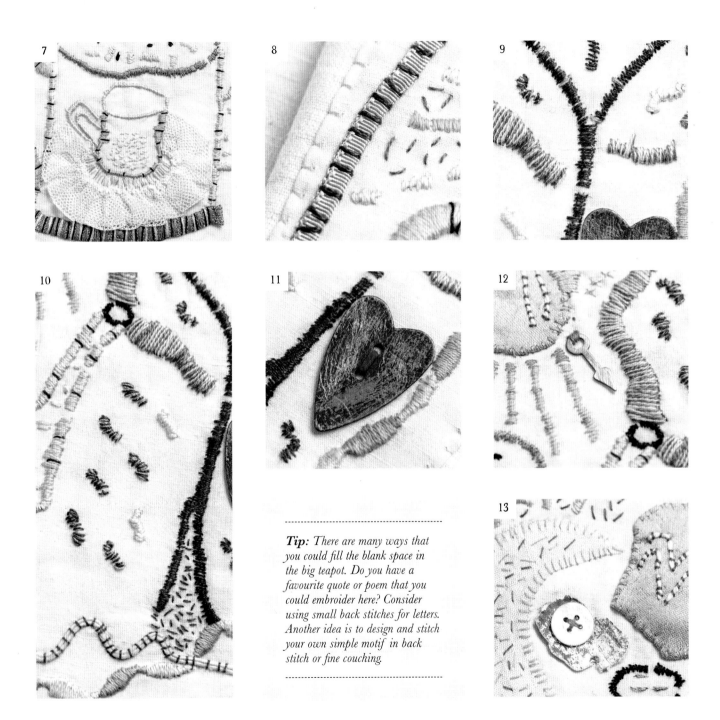

Tip: *There are many ways that you could fill the blank space in the big teapot. Do you have a favourite quote or poem that you could embroider here? Consider using small back stitches for letters. Another idea is to design and stitch your own simple motif in back stitch or fine couching.*

Winter page

Winter is upon us! This design features a
homely, festive scene. The main house is
surrounded by a winter garden of trees,
with a big star shining in the sky. This
design again has lots of texture: the house
has an appliquéd roof and appliqué is
also used for the lace sash, triangular
flags and doormat. Most of the motifs
are worked in satin stitch, but some are
couched. One tree has silver metal poppers
to represent twinkly lights, while the other
has raised seed stitches for baubles.

Winter page design

Think about how you might make this festive design personal to you. What will you add to the blank space inside the main house? How will you decorate the Christmas tree? Will there be gifts under the tree? Or stockings?

NOTE: By now you should have attached your Winter transfer design to your base fabric. For tips, tricks and inspiration refer back to 'Using the transfers'.

As with the Spring page, the roof of the house is appliquéd early on in the process and filled with straight stitches at a later date (**1**). You could also build the roof from lines of couching, raised seed stitches or small cross stitches.

Two strands of fine jute string are couched down to represent the lawn outside the festive house (**2**). To couch the string down, I used DMC Coton Perlé thread in colour 937. The ends of the string are left loose but at a later date I finished this section by tying a brass bell to one end of the string.

I wanted to keep the house simple and worked with red, white and pink tones to decorate it (**3**). A small scrap of red checked fabric is appliquéd on for the inner circle of the doormat (**4**). I tucked the edges under as I stitched it in place and then moved on to fill the rest of the doormat with satin stitches. The bright pink stitches were made using a vintage thread and the inner ones are built using one strand of DMC Mouliné thread in colour 842. To further decorate the house in a simple but stylish manner I added a lace sash, and little fabric flags hang from it (**3**). The ends of the lace are stitched down and discreet little stitches hold the main piece of lace in place. The flags are simply tiny scraps of fabric held in place with straight seed stitches. The flags are quite fragile, so I added them to the page as a final making stage.

The chimneys are filled in with satin stitch using one strand each of DMC Mouliné thread in colours 224 and 310 (**5**). The outside of the house is couched using one strand each of DMC Coton Perlé thread in colours 3033 and 758 (**6**).

Tip: *The blank area inside the house offers an opportunity to make this space personal to you. You could use fabric scraps to appliqué a person, little curtains, a door, or a festive wreath. You could also add some sparkly details using metallic threads, or even add some small beads or sequins.*

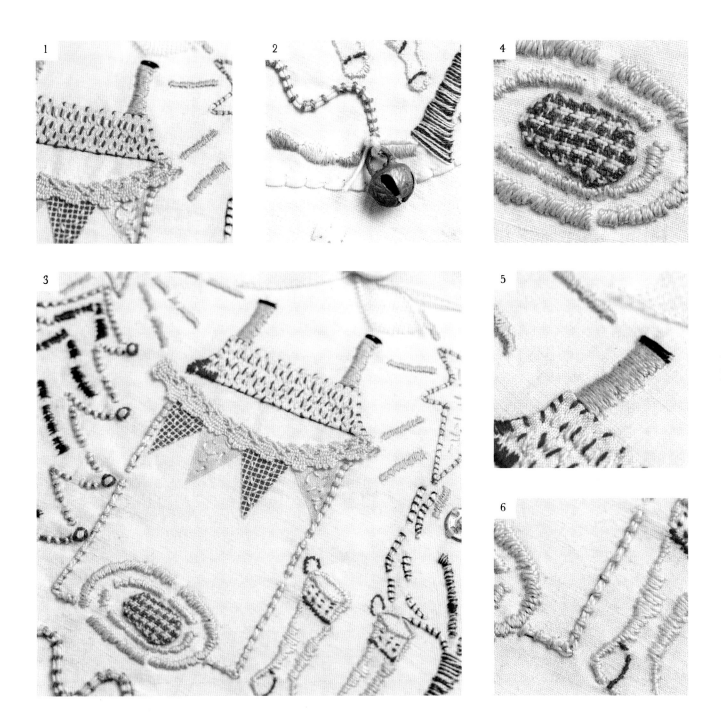

WINTER PAGE DESIGN

Above the house is a bow created from a piece of net ribbon (**7**). The bow is fixed in place with a linen button and a red stitch, worked with one strand of DMC Mouliné thread in colour 321.

This same red thread is used in the roof, the stockings, the Christmas trees baubles, and the red bucket that the Christmas tree sits in is finely satin stitched in this same shade of red.

I have carefully stitched a piece of fine lace (**8**) to the bottom left-hand border of my Winter page. What do you think you could use here? What do you have at home?

To build up the tree trunk and the main branches I ran satin stitches around them from the bottom of the trunk to the top of the branches (**9**). To do this, I used one strand each of DMC Mouliné thread in colours 3031 and 613. The two threads were worked running through my needle together to create this variegated colour effect.

To build up the tree's winter crown (**9**), I created a speckled effect by couching using DMC Coton Perlé thread in colour 3033 as the base thread. I then stitched over the base thread with small straight stitches using one strand of DMC Mouliné thread in colour 3031. This created a lovely, wintry feeling. I then stitched silver metal fasteners inside the tree (**10**). I wanted these shiny items to represent Christmas lights: the kind of lights that may be hung outside in the garden at this festive time of year.

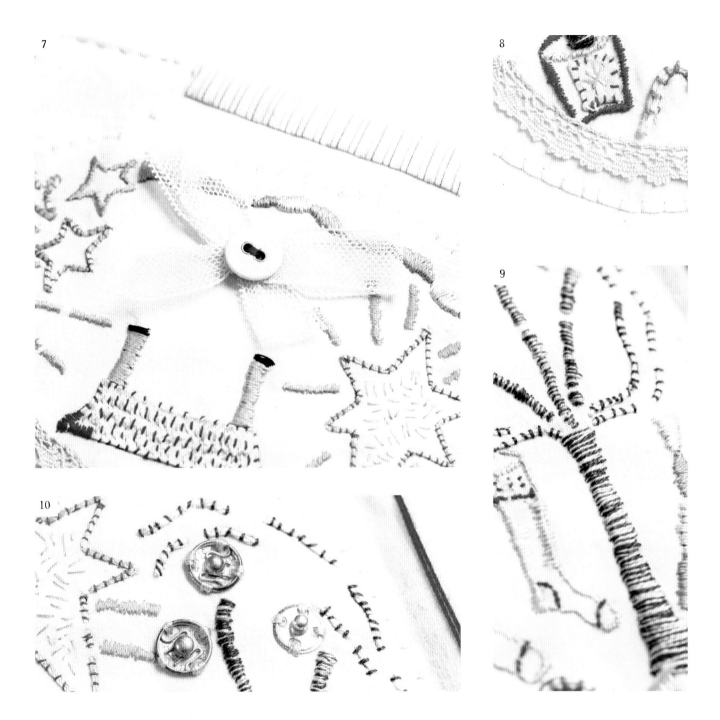

To embellish the Christmas tree (**11**), I first laid down DMC Coton Perlé thread in colour 937, then stitched back over this base thread using the same type of thread, but this time in colour 3033, using small straight stitches. The dark green area inside the Christmas tree was built up with small uneven satin stitches using one strand of DMC Mouliné thread in colour 890.

To create the baubles (**12**), I added raised seed stitches using one strand of DMC Mouliné thread in colour 613. They were then outlined with tiny back stitches in red thread.

Inside the red bucket that holds the Christmas tree, I appliquéd a tiny scrap of ivory silk fabric (**13**). This was the same fabric that I used for the roof. To finish this section I added a gold silk cross stitch.

The small stars above the Christmas tree (**14**) were mainly satin stitched very finely over both the star designs and the lines that project from the stars; however, three of the stars are couched. To create the couched stars, I laid down DMC Coton Perlé thread in colour 3033 and then worked little straight stitches back over this base thread in a variety of fine vintage threads.

For the large star to the right of the house (**15**), I once again used couching in vintage threads. The light rays that travel out from the star are satin stitch, worked with vintage threads but also using one strand of DMC Mouliné thread in colour 3852. I filled the big star with a scattering of small long seed stitches using found silk and shiny threads in yellow and blue.

To create the stockings (**16**), first I resized and traced the stocking template design from the back of this book. I then transferred my traced drawings by rubbing my traced pencil marks directly off onto my Winter page. I used two of the stocking motifs, one is deliberately slightly bigger than the other. I outlined the designs with fine satin stitch using one strand each of DMC Mouliné thread in colours 613 and 842, with the single strands worked individually. Finally, I added dashes of red to the stockings.

Extra embellishments

I really like the simplicity of this Winter page. It reminds me of how I like to decorate my own home around the festive season. To reflect this, I have kept further embellishments on the outside edges of this page to a minimum. The snippet of soft red fabric from a vintage patchwork quilt that I used on the Autumn page has travelled over to the Winter page, and is appliquéd to the top left-hand corner. I have added a cross-shaped stitch to this red patch, which was crafted using vintage threads. The design is supposed to be an abstract take on a gift-wrapped present.

A long patch of soft, stripy cotton fabric runs over the top edge of the page and again, this is also part of my Autumn page. On the top right-hand side of the page I have couched a star using vintage threads. The flowing string, which is couched down at the bottom of this page, is a continuation from the Autumn design. To finish, I have added a few patches of soft floral fabrics, which are also snippets from a vintage patchwork quilt.

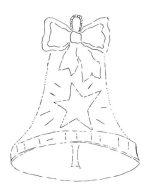

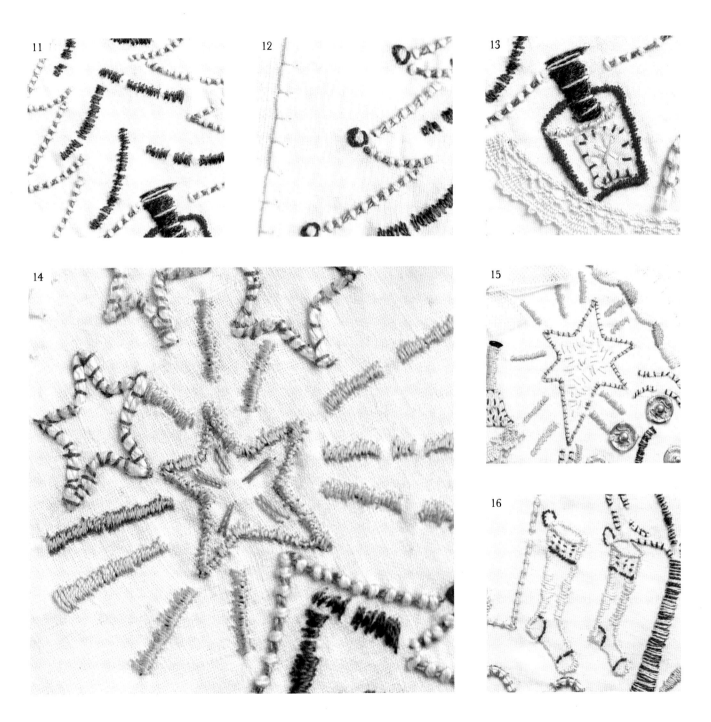

11 12 13

14 15

85

16

Inside back cover

This design, which is titled Pin Cushion, is intended for the journal's inside back cover. Think of it as a beautiful end page for your seasonal journal, which also serves a practical purpose as a place to store a few favourite pins and needles. It features satin stitch, couching and scattered appliqué, as well as scraps of vintage quilt, a piece of treasured tape measure and a charming, tiny brass safety pin.

Inside back cover design

How will you personalize this design? What treasure and precious details will you add to your pin cushion? Enjoy gathering together favourite items for this area and add them as a final stage of your personal making journey.

NOTE: By now you should have attached your inside back cover transfer design to your base fabric. For tips, tricks and inspiration refer back to 'Using the transfers'.

Really take time over this design, make it beautiful and highly decorated, but also think of this page as a useful and practical area for you to house your favourite pins and needles. This motif is designed to be a shrine to our mutual love of embroidery, fabric and thread. I hope that you will enjoy embellishing it as much as I have!

I worked up my pin cushion mainly using satin stitch. It is rich and full of pops of juicy colour. The base of the design was created by couching down a piece of ivory silk and securing it in place with small straight stitches, using a variety of vintage silk threads (**1**). How will you personalize this area of the design?

Much like in a collage, a snippet of pink fabric measuring tape is carefully secured in place at the centre of the design (**2**) with small black straight stitches. What will you fill this area with? A name or date could be stitched into this space, which would be perfect if you are making this project as a gift.

I worked the top edge of the pin cushion design (**2, 3**), building up the border using satin stitch. For this I used one strand of red and one strand of pink DMC Mouliné thread in colours 321 and 224. These two colours were threaded through my needle together and stitched at the same time, to create a variegated stitch style.

The pins and needles motifs (**3**) were built up with satin stitch using one strand each of DMC Mouliné thread in colours 648 and 310. I then used precious vintage threads to add colour to the tips of the pins.

For the thread colours that flow out from the needles (**3**), I used one strand each of DMC Mouliné thread in colours 321, 3852 and 924. I worked these colours in fine satin stitch using just one strand of thread to give these wobbly lines a sense of movement

Finally, I added some pins and needles from my collection (**4**) and a small scrap of vintage patchwork quilt, secured in place with a beautiful old brass safety pin (**3**). What trinkets or keepsakes will you add to this area?

For tips on how to finish this page and go about padding the completed pin cushion, please refer back to 'Attaching completed panels to a premade journal'.

Extra embellishments

To add further detail to this page, I have again used one of the small templates from the back of this book. This scissors motif sits at the bottom right of the page. I have also stitched a flowing needle and thread design that stretches across the top and left side of the page. The needle was stitched using one strand each of DMC Mouliné thread in colours 613 and 310. The needle has couched thread flowing from it. The couching was made using vintage threads. There is a piece of fine lace in a subtle pinky-brown tone stitched to the right-hand edge of the page along with a scattering of appliquéd patches. One linen patch has a vintage pearl button stitched to its centre (**5**). To finish, I have added some pieces of beautiful soft wool to tuck my needles into.

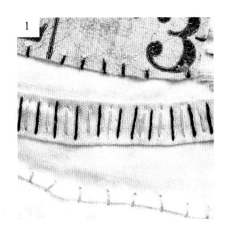

1

2

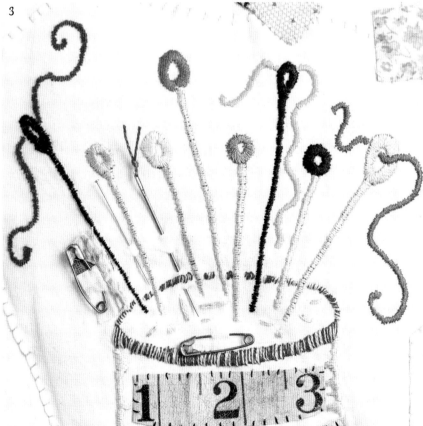

Tip: *Another idea for this page is to make the pin cushion into a pocket. If you want to do this, I suggest first creating a simple fabric pocket and then transferring the pin cushion motif onto it before embellishing the design. Finally, stitch the pocket into your journal.*

3

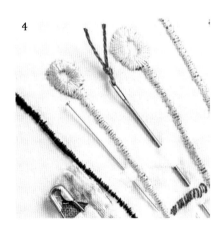

4

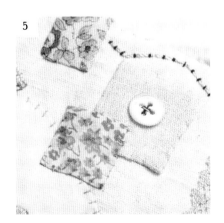

5

INSIDE BACK COVER DESIGN

Back cover

This design, titled Rosette, is intended for the journal's back cover. The simple circular border, with a statement bow at the top, allows space for you to add a personal touch of your choice – I couched my name, using the same colour for both the base thread and the whipped top thread. The tips of the pins are created using treasured old threads, while the bow is decorated with a vintage Suffolk puff/yoyo and linen button.

Back cover design

Take inspiration from my finely stitched name and lettering style as you carefully consider what you will place in the blank area inside the rosette design. How will you embellish this space in your own journal? Think of this design as the final stage of your making process.

NOTE: By now you should have attached your back cover transfer design to your base fabric. For tips, tricks and inspiration refer back to 'Using the transfers'.

It's important to sign your journal, and any artwork in general. I suggest adding your name to the back cover's rosette design; you could also add a date. Or, if the journal is a gift, you could add the recipient's name and a personal note.

Initially, I worked the main bow of the rosette (**1**), building up the shape using satin stitch. I used one strand of red and one strand of pink DMC Mouliné thread for this in colours 321 and 224. The two colours were threaded together through my needle and stitched at the same time. This creates a beautiful, variegated stitch style. To shade inside the bow (**1, 2**), I scattered small, straight seed stitches using single strands of DMC Mouliné thread in red and blue (colours 321 and 924). I worked the red thread and straight stitches first and then filled in between the red stitches with the blue thread using small straight stitches.

The rosette's pink border (**3, 5**) was built up using two strands of DMC Mouliné thread in colour 224 to create dense satin stitches. I then added a small appliquéd patch (**3**) to the right-hand side of the pink border. This small scrap of checked fabric is an absolute favourite of mine! What little details will you add to your final design?

I added a vintage Suffolk puff/yoyo (**4**) to the centre of my bow. The puff is secured with a linen button. Before attaching the puff, I stitched around its border with a variety of vintage threads. I used one strand of DMC Mouliné thread in colour 3852 to secure my button and the puff in place.

To fill the needle and the three pin motifs (**5**), I used one strand each of DMC Mouliné thread in colours 648 and 310. A variety of vintage threads were used to add colour to the tips of the pins. Do the same using colours from your own collection.

To finish, I stitched my name using finely couched lettering (**6**). I used one strand of DMC Mouliné thread in colour 924 as my base thread then one strand of the same blue thread was finely whipped back over the blue base thread in small, straight stitches. Finally I dotted the letter 'i' in my name with a raised seed stitch made from a vintage thread.

Extra embellishments

To add further embellishments to my back cover, I appliquéd on two of the small designs from the back of this book: the coffee pot and the bouquet. A chunk of blue running stitch made with a vintage thread anchors the bottom of the page. A small heart is couched down to the right of the rosette motif. A flower floats across the top of the page and is embroidered using mainly vintage threads. It has a beautiful, wavy couched stem and purple satin-stitched petals. An additional needle and thread is stitched to the bottom left of the page (**5**). Appliquéd fabric patches and cross-shaped stitches are scattered across the page to help complete it.

BACK COVER DESIGN

Additional templates

These smaller additional templates can be used in your seasonal fabric journal in any way you wish. You could also use them in future projects. You will see from the photos in this book that I have made myself a useful pin cushion brooch from the spool and needle design. It houses my pins and needles when I am sewing.

Enjoy adding these additional motifs into your journal in whatever way you find pleasing and practical. There is a wide range of designs to choose from, including an alphabet in both lower and upper case, plus a full set of number motifs. You could choose some to fill any of the blank spaces on the seasonal page transfer designs.

However, there are more designs than you will likely need for this journal, so keep them in mind for any upcoming personal projects. Think of them as a design bank that will be useful in the future. For example, some projects might be sparked off by this seasonal journal: why not consider making a beautiful pocket or envelope to house your completed fabric journal? You could use the additional motifs, alphabets and numbers to decorate a pocket, envelopes, box or bag. Another idea would be to make a bookmark for your journal, or page tabs and markers, and decorate them with the designs in this section. Have fun playing!

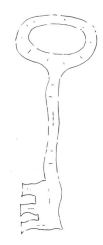

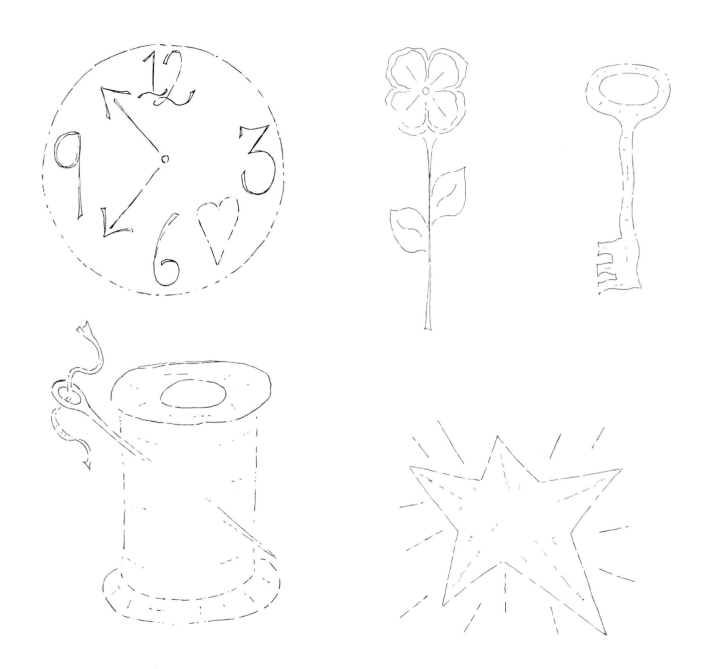

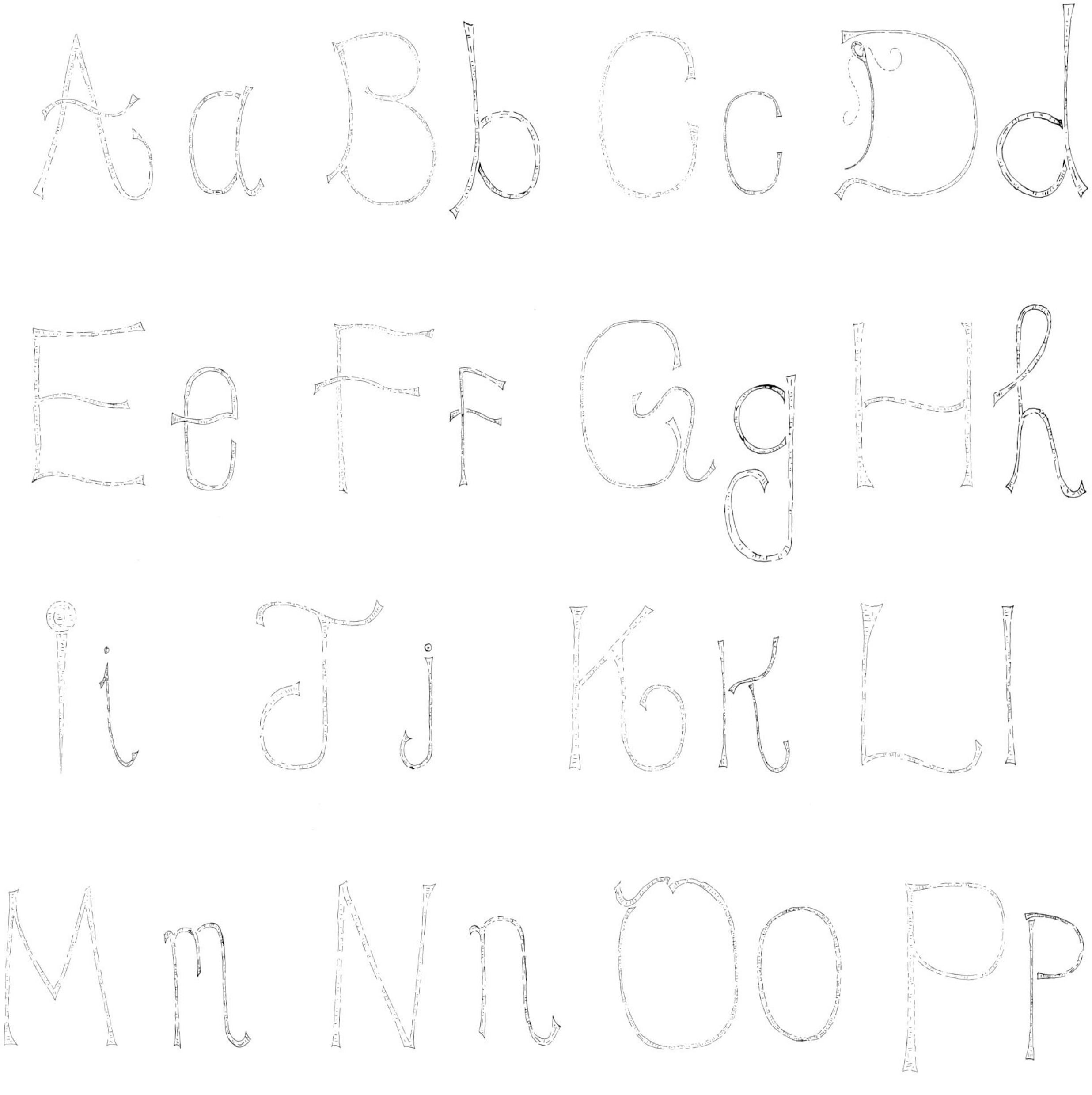

Aa Bb Cc Dd

Ee Ff Gg Hh

Ii Jj Kk Ll

Mm Nn Oo Pp

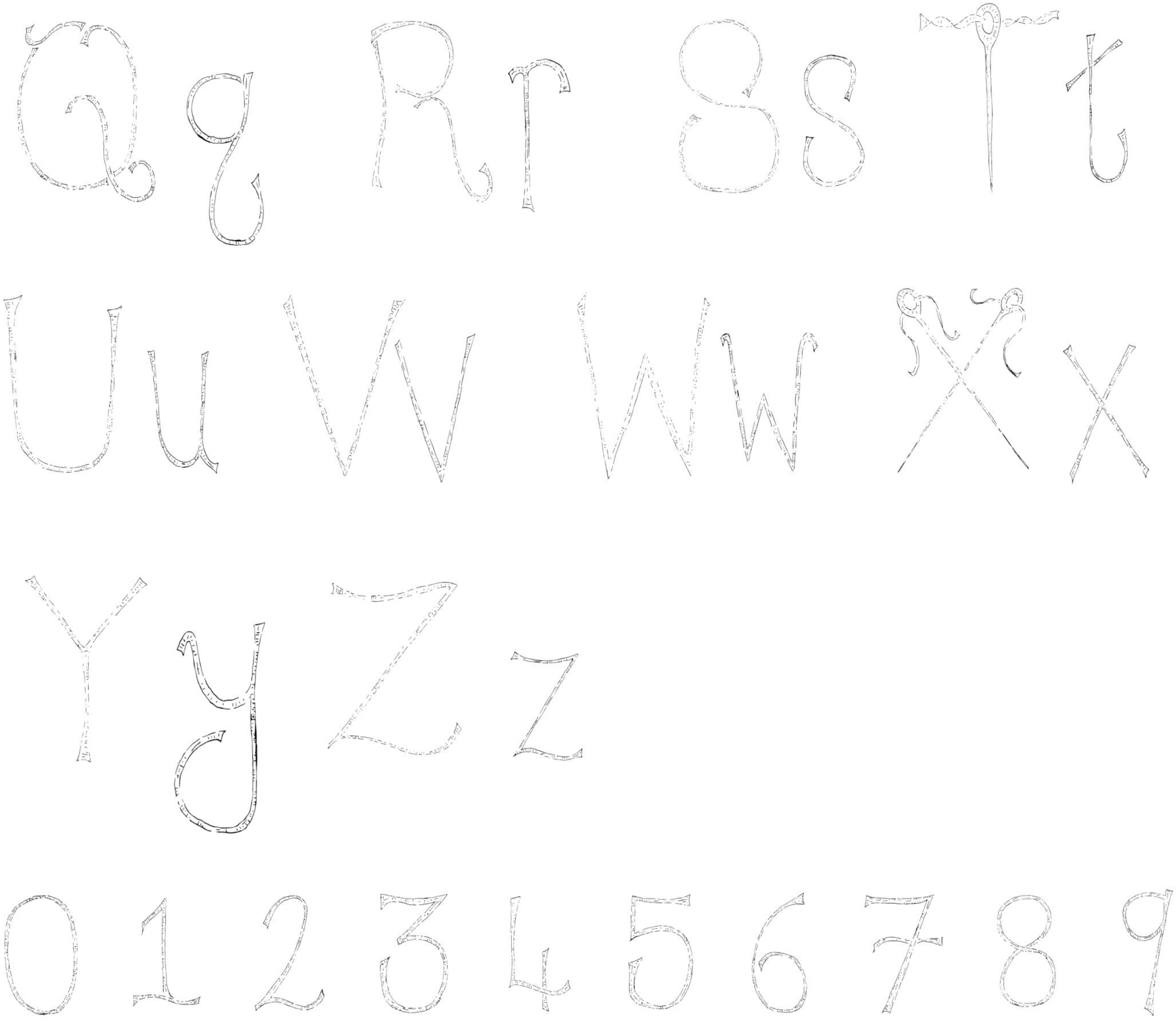

Qq Rr Ss Tt

Uu Vv Ww Xx

Yy Zz

0 1 2 3 4 5 6 7 8 9

Other ideas

At any stage of your fabric journal making process, I encourage you to enjoy adding assorted decorative details to your work. I am a huge fan of upcycling buttons by covering them, and crafting fabric bows from preloved fabric is also a great little project.

Making covered buttons

Covering buttons is a great way of using up both odd buttons and small fabric scraps. Completed buttons can be decorated with stitched words, personal initials or a favourite motif. They are perfect for adding detail to a fabric journal. Please note, flat and not too small buttons are the best ones to use. The ideal size is 3 x 3cm (1¼in) or slightly bigger, 5 x 5cm (2in). Smaller buttons can be too fiddly.

Step one: Choose a fabric to cover your button in. Don't use thick fabrics, velvets or wools. Linen, cotton and silk fabrics are best. Cut your chosen fabric into a circle approximately 1cm (⅜in) larger than your selected button.

Step two: Make a simple running stitch all the way around the edge of your fabric. Use a strong thread for this stitching. Then gather in your fabric around the button, securing it in place with some strong stitches. Cut off any unwanted pieces of fabric that appear after you have gathered the fabric. You will now have a lovely covered button.

Step three: If you wish to embroider onto your covered button, this should be done when you have freshly covered the button and not before. This is because the tension is perfect with the fabric stretched over the button – it's like a tiny stretched canvas ready for your needle and thread to slip into. Using a graphite pencil or erasable pen, lightly draw your design directly onto the front of your covered button.

Step four: Embroider your button in a stitch or stitches of your choice. If needed, you can refer bto my 'Hiding knots and top stitching' instructions.

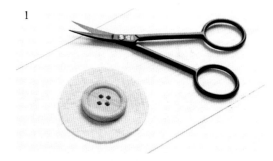

Making stitched bows

Making stitched bows is a great way of using up small, odd scraps of your favourite fabrics. They can be crafted in a variety of plain and printed fabrics. Once they're constructed, enjoy embellishing them with words of your choice, decorative stitches, or a beautiful button could be attached to the centre of your bow. Steer clear of both thick or very thin fabrics when making bows. Linens and cotton fabrics work best.

Step one: Cut a rectangle from your fabric measuring roughly 5 x 8cm (2 x 3¼in). The size you cut your fabric to will determine the final size of your completed bow. However, bear in mind that whatever size you want your bow to be you must add 1cm (⅜in) to each of the three raw edges as a hem. These three raw edges will be tucked under, before being stitched down neatly, to form the panel which will eventually become your bow. Fold your cut fabric in half and tuck the three raw edges under. Next, give this tucked-under fabric a good press with your iron and hold it in place with some pins.

Step two: Stitch around all four sides of your folded fabric with small straight stitches or with running stitches – either will work, and both will create a nicely finished edge. Once your edging stitches are complete, this is the time to decide whether to leave your bow plain or embellish it with running or seed stitches. This would add texture and/or a pattern. If you want to embroider words or a date, I would suggest waiting until step four in these instructions, when your bow will be complete and you can choose the spacing for such details.

Step three: Using a strong thread, work a line of running stitches directly through the middle of your currently flat double-sided fabric panel (or bow in progress) and proceed to gather in your fabric. Finish with a few strong and secure stitches to hold the gathers. Finally, press with your iron.

Step four: Add a button to the centre of your bow for detail. If you want to stitch words or a date onto your bow, this is the time to do so. Use small back stitches or fine couching for such details, and stitch neatly around any gathers in your bow. I find that the gathers and folds in my bows naturally guide me, and help me choose where to place stitched letters or numbers. Enjoy playing!

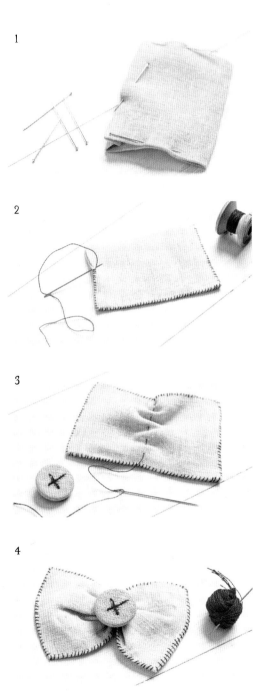

1

2

3

4

Knots

If you are preparing to sew onto a panel or motif that is allowed to have a messy reverse side, because it will eventually be stitched into your premade fabric journal, then normal knots are the best and most direct way to work. Before you start, remember to add a little beeswax to your thread. This wax will help your knot to stay tight and secure. To create a simple knot before sewing, I thread my needle and then tie a small knot at the tail end of the thread. The knot holds the thread securely as I start to stitch. You could also make a little anchor stitch though your fabric as well as a knot, just as you start. This is a good idea when working with fine, metallic or silk threads as small knots alone can still pull and jump through fabrics.

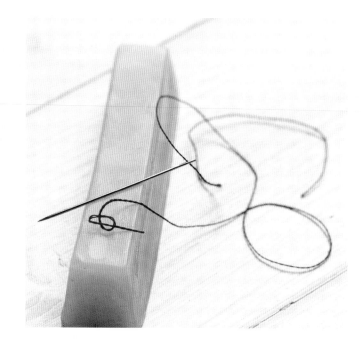

Fastening off

It's important to finish your stitching securely. Before you want to finish off your sewing, always make sure you have enough thread left in your needle to make several anchoring stitches on the reverse of your decorative work. Make the anchoring stitches, and then finish by looping your needle and thread through an existing stitch or stitches on the reverse of your work. Finally, cut your thread but always leave a little tail roughly 1cm (⅜in) in length. At a later date you can knot together any free trailing tail threads to give extra strength to your embroidery.

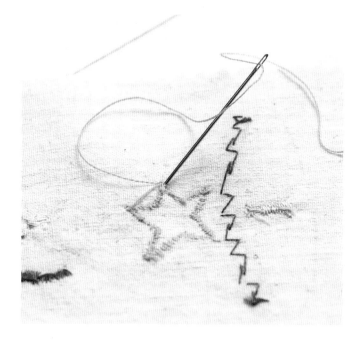

Hiding knots and top stitching

Top stitching into a premade fabric book is something I love to do, but I know it can be tricky and fiddly to both start off and finish your sewing using no visible knots. So here are some top tips from me.

Step one: To secure your thread with no visible knots, push the needle (with unknotted thread) into the base fabric, just skimming the top fabric. The needle should go slightly into the padding at this stage. Continue to push the needle and thread through in this way staying close to the surface, until the tail of your thread is lost in the fabric.

Step two: Now make a few very tiny anchoring stitches to secure the thread at your chosen starting point. You are now free to stitch from this anchored point.

Step three: Knots can also be hidden by pulling them into the hems of your fabric journal's covers and pages.

Step four: Alternatively, you could first anchor your thread with a knot and some small stitches to your base fabric or fabric book page and then hide the knot by covering it with a small appliquéd detail. The same thread that you have just attached to your fabric will be the thread that you now use to stitch your appliqué patch on with. Your knot will be hidden under your decorative patch. Get into the habit of hiding knots like this and top stitching neatly on to your premade fabric journal will become easy. Practice my tips and tricks using a piece of scrap fabric as a doodle cloth first if necessary.

1
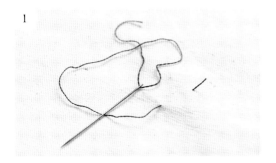

2

3

4
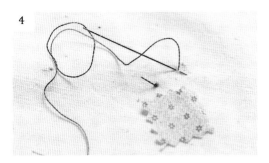

DMC colour codes

Resources

DMC Mouliné Spécial embroidery thread

White (colour code 613)

Beige (colour code 842)

Black (colour code 310)

Red (colour code 321)

Mid Green (colour code 3362)

Dark Green (colour code 890)

Moss Green (colour code 730)

Light Pink (colour code 224)

Dark Pink (colour code 407)

Yellow (colour code 3852)

Blue (colour code 924)

Pale Silver Grey (colour code 648)

Brown (colour code 3031)

DMC Coton Perlé embroidery thread

Red (colour code 321)

Mushroom White (colour code 3033)

Black (colour code 310)

Pink (colour code 758)

Green (colour code 937)

To view my collection of slow stitch projects, fabrics, needles, threads plus my masterclass dates and information, please visit:

www.jessiechorley.com

Suppliers

For new threads, I recommend:

www.dmc.com

www.anchorcrafts.com

www.sajou.fr

www.woolwarehouse.co.uk

Recommended scissors:

Premax 10769 Dressmaking Scissors – Soft Touch Collection

Premax F12050414MT – Embroidery/Sewing scissors, Teflon-coated Collection

Plain base fabrics

www.raystitch.co.uk

www.merchantandmills.com

About the author

Jessie Chorley is a London-based textile artist, specializing in contemporary illustrative embroidery and simple patching techniques. Born in Kent in 1980, she spent her childhood in North Wales. The traditional technical skills and hands-on approach that she celebrates in her work today were passed down to her from her own family of makers.

While still a student – studying for a BA in Fine Art Textile Practice at Goldsmiths College, London – she chose to dedicate her life to making beautiful things and, shortly after graduating, she set up her own business as a full-time artist, designer and maker. Over time, she has also become a tutor, social artist and author, as well as running a shop and studio selling her work in East London from 2007 to 2021.

Jessie now runs her business from her private South London studio. She regularly delivers masterclasses from there, as well as at venues worldwide.

Traditional hand embroidery, simple patchwork and printmaking are at the heart of Jessie's practice as an artist-maker. Needle and thread are her drawing tools. She uses them to create scenes and stories, combining stitched images and words, largely on preloved fabric.

Collecting is something that goes hand-in-hand with Jessie's making process. She is drawn to items that display marks of a previous life and often sources materials from antique markets, fairs and junk shops. Her ever-growing personal archive of 'found' items serves as her ongoing inspiration and is frequently her starting point for an artwork.

"I find beauty and inspiration in things that have been discarded or put to one side – fabric cut directly from pre-worn clothing is my most frequently used material. I also keep worn, damaged and stained garments, bags or purses and use these items as canvases for my stories to grow on and into.

"I use many motifs taken from everyday life, that the viewer will instantly recognize and be able to relate to. But my work is not linear in its approach to storytelling. It's a fragmented affair held together with scraps of memory, real-life events and symbolic motifs, all held in place with my many stitches."

Acknowledgments

Thank you to my publisher, David & Charles for inviting me to create this book, thanks in particular to Sarah Callard. Thank you to Samantha Staddon, for working with me to create such beautiful graphics and an overall design style for this book. Thank you to my editor Jessica Cropper. Thank you to Lindsay Kaubi and Marie Clayton for helping me to edit my words, ideas, thoughts and technical instructions throughout this book. Thank you to Jason Jenkins and Sarah Rowntree for working with me at my studio to create the photos in this book.

A special thank you, to my mum and fellow embroidery artist, Primmy Chorley. Thank you for giving me the unique rural Welsh childhood that nourished, nurtured and formed the start of the life that I live as an embroidery artist today.

Thank you to both Max Barstow and Cécile Landau for your expert editing skills, help and encouragement in the years before I was invited to write this book. You made crafting this book and especially editing my text a lot easier, you both gave me encouragement and confidence in writing. Thank you both.

Thank you to Valeria Giurdanella for your ongoing technical help. We travelled a long way together in graphic design days. I will always appreciate our time together and our friendship.

Finally, and very importantly, a huge thank you to my followers, friends and fellow stitchers, who continue to support my life as an artist, designer, tutor and author both online and in person here at my London studio. Thank you for continuing to support my creative life. Never stop stitching and making things with your hands and hearts.

Share your story

I cherish keeping in touch with you, my students, friends and fellow stitchers. I love seeing your personal versions of my projects come to life. Therefore I invite you to keep in touch with me during your seasonal stitching journey. How is your journal-making adventure going? What is your favourite part of the project? Tips for other makers? What is your favourite motif?

To keep me updated and to share your personal versions of this project, simply tag me on Instagram @jessiechorley, using the hashtag #jessiechorleyjournalwiththread

You can also email me images and technical questions via my website, www.jessiechorley.com

I hope that you enjoy your personal journey, knowing others are doing the same in many different corners of this world, either solo or in small friendship groups and sewing bees.

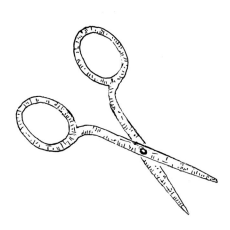

Index

A DAVID AND CHARLES BOOK
© David and Charles, Ltd 2024

David and Charles is an imprint of David and Charles, Ltd
Suite A, Tourism House, Pynes Hill, Exeter, EX2 5WS

Text and Designs © Jessie Chorley 2024
Layout and Photography © David and Charles, Ltd 2024

First published in the UK and USA in 2024

A catalogue record for this book is available from the British Library.

ISBN-13: 9781446313060 hardback
ISBN-13: 9781446313084 EPUB
ISBN-13: 9781446313077 PDF

This book has been printed on paper from approved suppliers and
made from pulp from sustainable sources.

Printed in China through Asia Pacific Offset for:
David and Charles, Ltd
Suite A, Tourism House, Pynes Hill, Exeter, EX2 5WS

10 9 8 7 6 5 4 3 2 1

Publishing Director: Ame Verso
Senior Commissioning Editor: Sarah Callard
Managing Editor: Jeni Chown
Editor: Jessica Cropper
Project Editors: Lindsay Kaubi and Marie Clayton
Head of Design: Anna Wade
Designer: Laura Woussen
Pre-press Designer: Susan Reansbury
Illustrations and Styling: Jessie Chorley
Art Direction: Sarah Rowntree
Photography: Jason Jenkins
Production Manager: Beverley Richardson

David and Charles publishes high-quality books on a wide range of
subjects. For more information visit www.davidandcharles.com.

Share your makes with us on social media using #dandcbooks and
follow us on Facebook and Instagram by searching for @dandcbooks.

Layout of the digital edition of this book may vary depending on
reader hardware and display settings.

Iron on transfers

Here are the iron on transfers. Enjoy using them together with the technical
instructions, tips and creative ideas within this book. Make them personal to your story,
take inspiration from my version of these embellished designs, and have fun!

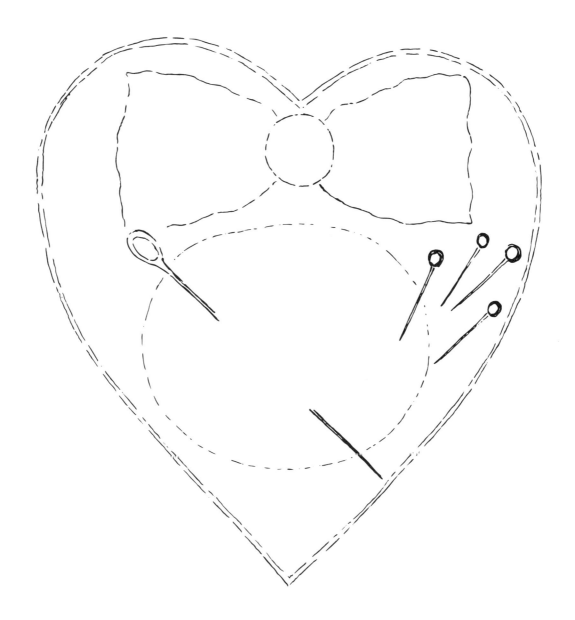

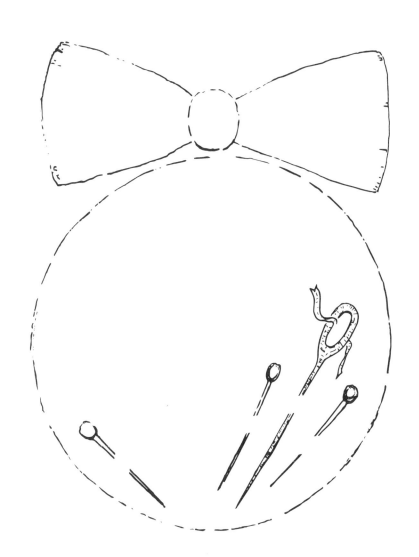